THE LAST SUPPER

The Last Supper
Conversations That Led to the Cross

The Last Supper
978-1-7910-3738-3
978-1-7910-3739-0 *eBook*

The Last Supper: DVD
978-1-7910-3742-0

The Last Supper: Leader Guide
978-1-7910-3740-6
978-1-7910-3741-3 *eBook*

Also by Will Willimon

The Church We Carry:
Loss, Leadership, and the Future of the Church

Changing My Mind:
The Overlooked Virtue for Faithful Ministry

Heaven and Earth:
Advent and the Incarnation

THE LAST SUPPER

Conversations That Led to the Cross

WILL WILLIMON

Abingdon Press | Nashville

The Last Supper
Conversations That Led to the Cross

Library of Congress Control Number: 2025946594
978-1-7910-3738-3

Sketch at the end of each chapter is by the author.

Book cover description for *The Last Supper: Conversations That Led to the Cross* by Will Willimon. The top half shows the title in large white capital letters, with "THE" above a black line and "LAST SUPPER" stacked below. The background features a colorful, abstract illustration of Jesus and several disciples at the table, rendered with overlapping geometric shapes in vibrant shades of blue, red, orange, green, and yellow. Below the artwork, a beige strip holds the subtitle in black serif text. The author's name appears at the bottom in large white serif letters on a dark, multicolored background.

MANUFACTURED IN THE UNITED STATES OF AMERICA

When the time came, Jesus took his place at the table, and the apostles joined him. He said to them, "I have earnestly desired to eat this Passover with you before I suffer. I tell you, I won't eat it until it is fulfilled in God's kingdom." After taking a cup and giving thanks, he said, "Take this and share it among yourselves. I tell you that from now on I won't drink from the fruit of the vine until God's kingdom has come." After taking the bread and giving thanks, he broke it and gave it to them, saying, "This is my body, which is given for you. Do this in remembrance of me." In the same way, he took the cup after the meal and said, "This cup is the new covenant by my blood, which is poured out for you.

"But look! My betrayer is with me; his hand is on this table."

Luke 22:14-21

View a complimentary session
of Will Willimon's
The Last Supper

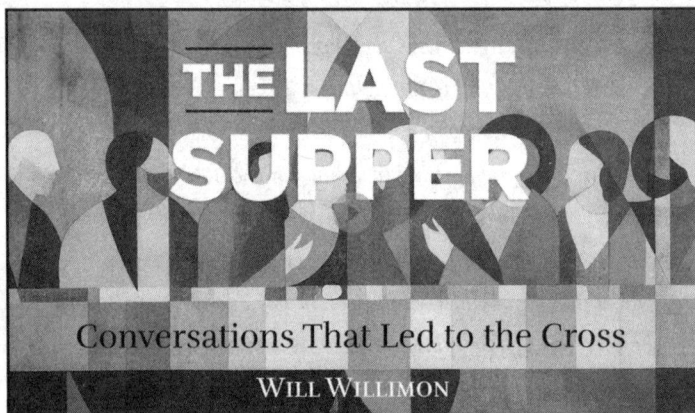

Scan the QR code below or visit
https://bit.ly/thelastsupper
_session1.

CONTENTS

Introduction
PALM SUNDAY
The Journey to the Table

Sure, Jesus's teaching, healing, and preaching drew crowds in the Galilean outback. But how will Jesus fare in Jerusalem, the capital city?

On Palm Sunday he barges right into town uninvited, unwanted even, parading in public, up front in his intentions to claim the city as his own (Matthew 21:1-11; Luke 19:28-44). We shouldn't be surprised by his politics. Never did Jesus begin a parable, "A personal relationship with me is like . . ." It was always, "The kingdom of heaven is similar to . . . " "God's kingdom," politics Jesus-style, is the theme of most of his parables.

Conquering your precious heart or solving your personal problems are too small a goal for Jesus's royal aspirations. As John puts it, "God so loved the world that he gave his only Son . . ." (John 3:16). The world, the whole world, more than your heart or even your zip code. On Palm Sunday Jesus mixes religion with politics, takes it to the streets, in a public dispute with Caesar over who's in charge.

At last. "Hosanna! Hail, king!" (Luke 19:28-40).

But who thinks "king" when you see this itinerant country rabbi astride a borrowed donkey, his motley crew tagging along behind him on Palm Sunday?

Looking back on this scene, Matthew remembered an ironic promise by the prophet Zechariah:

> Rejoice greatly, Daughter Zion.
> Sing aloud, Daughter Jerusalem.
> Look, your king will come to you.
> He is righteous and victorious.
> He is humble and riding on an ass,
> on a colt, the offspring of a donkey.
> (Zechariah 9:9; Matthew 21:4-5)

A king, "victorious" as well as "humble," a triumphal royal entry on a wobbling, skinny donkey? Parabolic paradox, oxymoron, joke, and riddle, not spoken but enacted on Palm Sunday.

Along the road and at the table Jesus told so many riddles; he now dramatically becomes the greatest conundrum of all. Look! There's your king, righteous, victorious . . . riding on an ass, a rented one at that.

We want Jesus to get off that ridiculously modest donkey and swagger right up to the palace, plop down on the imperial throne, seize a royal scepter, and begin to issue executive decrees for the liberation of Judea.

Instead, Jesus goes to the temple, heals some sick people, then turns over the tables, causing chaos, provoking indignant uproar among the temple-going righteous, accusing us of having made the holy place "a hideout for crooks." Just about the meanest thing anybody has ever said about us clergy (Luke 19:46).

"My kingdom is not from here," Jesus told Pilate at the trial. Here, where all monarchs prop up their power with an army, here, where political strong-arming is the only way to get any good done, where people are admired, not for their love and mercy, but for their ability to coerce, enforce, build walls, make threats, and anybody who sheds an empathetic tear is dismissed as a wimp. Here.

Then there, at week's end, at the table, in his last meal before execution, all Jesus did was to host a modest meal during which he offered a cup of wine, "This cup is the new covenant by my blood, which is poured out for you" (Luke 22:20).

This, God's promised salvation?

King on a donkey. An adoring crowd turns into a murderous mob, a preacher who lives and dies what he says, God nailed to a cross, a mighty Savior who shares his last meal with sinful betrayers who are also his best friends?

We wanted him to unfurl a battle flag, storm Jerusalem, and set up a new messianic King of David government. Instead, he gave us a simple supper of bread and wine with a bunch of disappointing, simpleton disciples.

But I get ahead of myself.

As we stumble after him on the road to that last fateful meal, Jesus tells stories, riddles. During the forty-day trek from Ash Wednesday to Maundy Thursday, story after story, Jesus reveals where he is taking us, unveiling, preparing us for the table in the upper room when he will solve the riddles and show and tell all.

"Who are you?" we wondered. "Where are we headed?" Jesus answered, but indirectly, with pithy little stories that teased, cajoled, upset, made us smile, befuddled, disoriented, or sometimes smacked us up beside the head. "A farmer scattered seed . . ." "Hear the one about the shepherd who lost a sheep?" "Two people went to the temple to pray . . ."

The gospel is truth we can't tell ourselves. Nobody is born knowing the good news, nor has anybody ever drifted toward the conviction that a man—tortured to death by a consortium of religious and governmental leaders, hosting his disappointing disciples for a final Maundy Thursday meal, hanging from a cross in agony on Good Friday, forgiving those who nailed him there— is the whole truth about God.

Want to get close to Jesus? You'll have to sit for story time with him.

Matthew and Mark say Jesus said nothing except in parables (Matthew 13:34; Mark 4:34). Over half of everything Luke quotes from Jesus is in parables or, as we'll name some of them, riddles.

Humanity's oldest riddle is from Sumer, six thousand years ago: "What building do you enter blind and exit sighted?"

Answer: "A school."

These days we prefer truth handed to us on a platter, three obvious points, six knock-down principles for a stress-free life, four takeaways, three irrefutable reasons to get out of bed in the morning, five doctrines you must believe if you are to be a Christian. Biblical fundamentals.

Sorry, that's not Jesus's way. If his good news could be encapsulated in easy-to-remember general principles, he would have. Instead, he told stories as a sly stratagem to make his story yours.

"Jesus came into Galilee announcing God's good news, saying, 'Now is the time! Here comes God's kingdom! Change your hearts and lives, and trust this good news!'" (Mark 1:14-15).

"Tell us, what's it like when God's kingdom comes, God's will is done on earth as it is in heaven?"

Jesus responds, "Try this. Somebody lies wounded, dying in a ditch in need of saving . . . it can be compared to an invitation to a great feast . . . a woman lost a coin and . . ." Working from everyday experiences of a world we know, Jesus . . . reveals a world we can't know (i.e., the kingdom of God or, as Matthew describes it, "kingdom of heaven") without listening to his story.

A warning before you get too far down the road with these riddles: God's realm is so different from our kingdoms that when Jesus is revealing, sometimes it feels like he's concealing.

As Jesus told Pontius Pilate on that bleak Friday, "My kingdom isn't from here" (John 18:36), so it's bound to sound strange when you first hear of it. Still, you can trust Jesus: he's telling you this story because he wants to open your eyes so that you can see the good news for yourself.

A parable is a GPS taking you to a new world that's God's rather than the fake world in which we bedded down.[1] Want to join Jesus at his table? All you've got to do is "Listen!" (Matthew 15:10).

Sure, Jesus wants to connect with us, but he refuses to put his truth on the bottom shelf. Good news: Your misunderstanding and incomprehension won't stop him from talking. When you respond to some of his more opaque stories with, "I'm sorry, I don't get it," what does he say? "Try this: The realm of God could be compared to a father who had two sons, both pains in the neck, though in different ways . . ."

Better than understanding Jesus is to be at table with Jesus. Rather than boasting, "I got it!" it's better to be able to say, at a parable's end, "Jesus just got me."

Maybe you come to church seeking confirmation for what you already know, and then Jesus throws a curveball of a parable and you find yourself dislocated, subverted, pushed on stage as a character in Jesus's drama of salvation, made citizen of a kingdom not from here. On the basis of nothing but a story.

If you journey with Jesus as he heads toward his last meal you'll have to put up with his riddles.

What kind of Son of God, Prince of Peace, Savior of the World would end up at supper, the night before his death, with a cluster of losers, promising them a place at the table in his coming kingdom?

This book is your answer.

Will Willimon

Chapter 1
SOWING, SEEKING, FINDING

Heard the one about the dinner party messed up by Jesus?

Simon the Pharisee—a pious, biblically knowledgeable religious leader—invited Jesus to dinner (Luke 7:36). In the Gospels, Pharisees like Simon are depicted as religious experts who can't stand Jesus; yet they persist in inviting him into their homes for supper! Maybe they hope to trick this rural rabbi into saying something stupid that can be used against him with the Romans. Yet in every case, Jesus turns the tables on his pharisaical critics with parables.

Let's make that evening at Simon's a fancy dinner party, sophisticated, expensive, and snobby. A blessing is offered. (Our custom of saying grace before meals comes from the Jews for whom, once the food is blessed, every meal is sacred.) Scarcely has the Mogen David been poured and the brisket unveiled than a "woman of the city" barges in mid-soiree. She falls all over Jesus, anointing and massaging his feet with sweet ointment, letting her hair down and causing an uproar by bathing Jesus's "feet with her tears." (Yes, "letting down her hair" meant the same thing then as now.) Assorted "well, I never" and "outrageous" among the horrified guests.

"When the Pharisee who had invited Jesus saw what was happening, he said to himself [smirking, loud enough for everybody at the table to hear], if this man were a prophet, he would know what kind of woman is touching him. He would know that she is a sinner" (Luke 7:39).

Some prophet, this Jesus, allowing this sinful woman to make such a scene, and at the table too. We aren't told the "sin" of this woman who "is touching him" (Greek: *haupto*, "touch," also "caress," "fondle"). Luke just says that she's a "woman of the city," leaving the rest to your prurient imagination.

Showing not the slightest interest in the shamelessly intruding woman's alleged sinfulness, Jesus smacks his religiously offended host with a riddle: "Someone owed a loan shark a hundred bucks [back in those days a dollar was worth something] and another guy owed fifty. The predatory lender forgave both debts! Now think hard Mr. Religious-know-it-all, which debtor would be the more grateful?" (Luke 7:42).

"I suppose, I guess you could say, probably, the one who was most forgiven?" (Luke 7:43) replies the embarrassed host, muttering, *Whose bright idea was it to invite this pushy preacher to dinner?*

Jesus turned to Simon, "Do do you see this woman?" Jesus asks. Of course not. Women were invisible at such occasions, particularly a "woman of the city." Jesus contrasts her ardor, kissing, anointing, weeping, and affectionate *haupto* with the dispassionate, dignified, detached, virtue signaling, but now humiliated, Pharisee.

As Jesus puts the screws to Simon, all the guests show sympathy for the plight of their host: "Who is this person that even forgives sins?" (Luke 7:49). Another dinner party ruined by Jesus and his riddles.

Leaving the Pharisee's stuffy table a shambles, Jesus and his merry band hit the road. Along the way, his stories continue. The word *parable* comes from the Greek, meaning "throw out," "toss." Why pitch these curve-ball riddles toward us? To reveal the "mysteries of God's kingdom" (Luke 8:9-10).

But God's realm isn't that easy to see. Maybe it's a mystery because the only kingdoms we know are the USA, UAR, UK, Tesla, Walmart, or Costco. Undeterred by our incomprehension, Jesus keeps pitching parables:

> He spoke to them in a parable: "A farmer went out to scatter his seed. As he was scattering it, some fell on the path where it was crushed, and the birds in the sky came and ate it. Other seed fell on rock. As it grew, it dried up because it had no moisture. Other seed fell among thorny plants. The thorns choked the young plants. Still other seed landed on good soil. When it grew, it produced one hundred times more grain than was scattered." As he said this, he called out, "Everyone who has ears should pay attention."
>
> (Luke 8:4-8)

Though we're all ears, we're grateful when, "His disciples asked him what this parable meant" (Luke 8:9).

Let's see if we've gotten your drift, Jesus: "The seed is God's word" and the parable describes what becomes of God's word once it's broadcast. Couple of questions: Why would any sane sower cast seed *on a road?* For that matter, who sows seed "on the rock" or "among thorny plants"? Seed so sloppily sown is of course "choked by the concerns, riches, and pleasures of life" (Luke 8:14).

Concern for friends and family, the achievement of a comfortable, secure income, enjoyment of leisure and recreation. Are these not good things? What chokes the seed is not evil, bad, sinful things, but "concerns, riches, and pleasures of life." Ironic, huh?

Even though I'm no great shakes as a gardener, seems to me that a great deal of good seed is being wasted here.

A farmer carefully removed all rocks and weeds from the soil, turned up the earth six inches deep, spaced neat furrows a foot apart, carefully covering each seed with a half inch of dirt? No! To hell with the asphalt, rocks, and weeds. Just sling that seed!

With such sloppy sowing, are you surprised there is farming failure? Most of this parable reports in detail the disappointing outcome.

Can you guess why the Sower is most preachers' favorite parable?

In five decades of ministry, nobody has said, "I'm not listening to your sermon because I don't believe there is a God." No. The forces that defeated my listeners are not their intellectual reservations about God but rather choking on assorted "concerns, riches, and pleasures of life."

"What's your greatest challenge in youth ministry?" I asked a youth pastor. He leaned under his desk and pulled out a soccer ball. "It's this. Our parents would rather their children learn soccer than Jesus."

I averaged preaching fifty sermons a year. Yet when asked, my listeners could remember no more than two or three. If "God's word" is "the seed" that's broadcast, a lot of seed is being wasted. At least when I'm slinging the seed from my pulpit.

What's the major reason given for leaving the pastoral ministry? A counselor of pastors replied, "It's the drip, drip of a gradually draining church. The daily, weekly, relentless meager results. Unremitting failure wears 'em down."

"She could'a been an attorney. Got a full scholarship to law school. Brilliant. Now she's stuck at a little country church, attendance, grand total of thirty," said her disappointed father. "Damn, what a waste."

Or . . . *is it an amazing harvest?* The curious thing is that Jesus doesn't characterize this as a farming disaster. The Sower has a surprise ending. "Still other seed landed on good soil. When it grew, it produced one hundred times more grain than was scattered." Jesus focuses us on the seed that succeeded rather than the seed that failed to germinate. While most of the scattered seed was wasted, more grain was produced, a hundred times more, than was lost in the reckless sowing. It's a miracle.

The Sower just loves to sow, slinging seed with abandon, casting good seed into seemingly hopeless contexts, undeterred by the prospect of farming failure, focusing upon the seed that bears fruit rather than the seed that fails.

Therein is our hope.

He had flunked out of college. Then the drugs and the DUI. Two weeks jail time. "So sad," said everybody at church. "After all his parents did for him, look how low he has sunk."

But nobody's story is over until Jesus says it's over. He will have the last word; loves to make surprise endings. I'll never forget the Sunday when the young man showed up, looking a bit sheepish, yes, but also bright and hopeful about a new beginning. For the first time in a long time he looked great. New job. Life going well. Volunteered to help in the food pantry next week.

Back in the congregation every Sunday thereafter.

Thank the Lord his story didn't end as we feared. What happened? He explained it to me one morning over coffee: "I was at this rock concert. Wasn't thinking about God. Trying hard not to think about anything. And in one of the songs, I heard the word, 'Why?' That's all. Kept ringing in my ears. 'Why?'

"Well, on the way home that night my girlfriend asked, out of nowhere, 'Why do you keep hurting yourself when God has given you so much?' I began to weep. Couldn't stop. Well, one thing led to another and, long story short, I'm back. Born again and all that."

Sure, a lot of good seed goes to waste. But Jesus won't let Almighty Death have the last word. Just one little seed, one word slung from the hand of the Sower, and there's miraculous harvest.

In the Gospel of John, speaking of his impending death, Jesus told sorrowing disciples a riddle: "I assure you that unless a grain of wheat falls into the earth and dies, it can only be a single seed. But if it dies, it bears much fruit" (John 12:24). Jesus, the "seed" cast down into death on a cross on Friday, a life wasted. Surprise! Unexpected, abundant harvest by Sunday.

I asked a teacher of elementary school teachers what's the most important characteristic for educators. She replied, "A good teacher must be in love with sowing the seed but doesn't need to be around for the harvest."

I ran right back to my class at Duke Divinity School and told that to my seminarians. Sling that seed with abandon, confident that the harvest is God's business. (Fun fact: *seminary* comes from the Latin, "seedbed," a school where seeds are slung that might bear fruit in future ministry.)

"Sadly, my daughter, who grew up in this church, loved the youth group and all that. But when she went off to college, she left the faith. Says she doesn't believe all this stuff and she's not a Christian."

"Not a Christian, *yet,*" I corrected. "You tell her to be careful. Take care what she reads, to whom she listens, where she walks. There's a reckless Sower out there, eagerly slinging seed her way. None of us is safe from the seed taking root in the heart and . . ."

No corner of the earth is dismissed as unfertile ground, and nothing shall defeat so generously scattered secrets determined to go public. Though the word germinates in the hearts of only a few, from those in whom it takes root, it bears abundant harvest. Nine-out-of-ten average Americans may listen, shrug their shoulders and hear nothing. But the Sower, who with such delight wildly, recklessly, graciously slings the seed, marvels at the harvest, otherwise known as your church, your life.

Only a small portion of the whole town will be gathered at your church this coming Sunday. Jesus's riddle suggests that it's a wonder that anybody is there, considering all of Satan's distractions, the "concerns, riches, and pleasures of life" that make hearing the word so hard for so many.

Jesus's truth is not to be safely tucked away in our hearts for safekeeping. It's to be broadcast into all the world. We're not to judge the potential receptivity of the soil unto which the seed is slung. Working with the Sower, our job is simply to join in Christ's exuberant slinging of seed, not to be discouraged when his peculiar kingdom truth fails to take root or folks just don't get Jesus's jokes. Go ahead, assistant sower, sling that seed.

Only twelve sat at table with Jesus at the Last Supper. Yet look at the harvest.

"Turning to the disciples, he said privately, 'Happy are the eyes that see what you see. I assure you that many prophets and kings wanted to see what you see and hear what you hear, but they didn't'" (Luke 10:23-24). We, his miraculous harvest, we happy few listening to Jesus's riddles, and in hearing him, see him more clearly, love him more dearly, so that we can follow more nearly.

Then Luke plays one of Jesus's greatest hits (Luke 10:25-37).

Mr. Me-Love-Bible-Better-Than-You swaggers up and asks a question meant to stump the Rabbi. (The Common English Bible version calls him a "legal expert" but, due to some negative experiences I've had with attorneys, I prefer the traditional "lawyer." That offends the jurists among you? Sue me.)

"Teacher," he said, "what must I do to gain eternal life?" (Luke 10:25).

Good one. Even though a recent Pew poll says that most Americans believe in some vague, heavenly future after death, a much smaller proportion believe that this "Teacher" who taught through riddles is the whole truth about God. Keep the conversation ethereal, spiritual, and fuzzily focused on the distant future.

Jesus, no fan of "legal experts" brushes him off with, "All of us Jews already know the answer: *You must love the Lord your God with all your heart, with all your being, with all your strength, and with all your mind, and love your neighbor as yourself"* (Luke 10:27; Deuteronomy 6:5; Leviticus 19:18).

"Do this and you will live" (Luke 10:28).

Undeterred, the expert who "wanted to prove that he was right" asked, "Yeah, yeah, but who is this 'neighbor' that I'm to love as much as I love me?" Jesus is backed into a corner where he'll be forced to distinguish between those who are worthy of neighborliness and those who are not. Where to draw the line? The deserving poor from the undeserving? Even Jews with whom we have doctrinal disagreements? Maybe. Roman occupation forces. Never! Those lousy, unfaithful, mixed-race Samaritans? Not a chance. Come on Jesus, show us your list of approved neighbors so we can have a debate over who's worthy to be my neighbor.

And Jesus answers with (what else?) a story:

A man went down from Jerusalem to Jericho. He encountered thieves, who stripped him naked, beat him up, and left him near death. Now it just so happened that a priest was also going down the same road. When he saw the injured man, he crossed over to the other side of the road and went on his way. Likewise, a Levite came by that spot, saw the injured man, and crossed over to the other side of the road and went on his way.

A Samaritan, who was on a journey, came to where the man was. But when he saw him, he was moved with compassion. The Samaritan went to him and bandaged his wounds, tending them with oil and wine. Then he placed the wounded man on his own donkey, took him to an inn, and took care of him. The next day, he took two full days' worth of wages and gave them to the innkeeper. He said, "Take care of him, and when I return, I will pay you back for any additional costs." What do you think? Which one of these three was a neighbor to the man who encountered thieves?

(Luke 10:30-36)

Wait a minute! I asked, "To whom ought *I* be neighborly?"

Jesus turns the tables on the lawyer, flipping the question into, "*Which of these three was a neighbor* to the man dying in the ditch?"

"I suppose, I guess, perhaps it's the . . . Samaritan," mumbles the lawyer.

"Can't heeear you," joshes Jesus.

The neighbor is the lousy, despisedly rich, unfaithful, half-breed . . . merciful . . . Samaritan. Not, to whom should I be a neighbor but who among the unlikely and despised has been a neighbor to me?

"But when he saw him, he was moved with compassion." The despised Samaritan was neighbor to the one in need, even though he didn't even know him and had nothing in common with him.

"Then don't stand around idly shooting the theological breeze, go and do likewise," says Jesus.[2]

(Would Jesus say to religious expert me, "All this writing and reading! Who needs another book on the Last Supper? *Go! Do!*")

This exchange began with the lawyer's question, "What should I do to gain eternal life?" Jesus's response suggests that "eternal life" isn't something we win someday after we die; it is life available here, now, whenever we obey Jesus's command to "go" and "do."

In my part of the world, ask folks, "Who's a Christian?" and they will likely respond, "A Christian is somebody who has accepted Jesus Christ as their personal Savior so that when they die they get to go to heaven."

Hear any of that in Luke 10?

What impresses me this time through this beloved (shocking?) parable is not just that the Samaritan stopped and cared, heck, I would have done that. It was the way he cared: extravagance and recklessness akin to a careless Sower slinging seed. Most of the verses in the parable are consumed with the Samaritan's effusive, costly, merciful actions.

The Samaritan took time for the man in the ditch. A risk, since the same brigands who beat the man within an inch of his life could also be waiting to mug the victim's savior. Ripping up his expensive suit and bandaging the man's "wounds, tending them with oil and wine," then placing the wounded man on the leather seats of his Jag, carrying him to an inn for long-term care, then taking two full days' worth of wages and giving it all to the innkeeper saying, "Take care of him, and when I return, I will pay you back for any additional costs."

This isn't a story about pausing to allow a victim to use your cell phone to call the highway patrol; it's a story about otherwise good people passing by and a bad Samaritan being actively, systemically, resourcefully, extravagantly merciful to a man in a ditch who was as good as dead.

Know anybody who extravagantly, wastefully, recklessly risked being a victim, mercifully giving away everything he had, even his own life, for a bunch of good-as-dead, down-in-the-ditch strangers?

Even from the cross on which we hung him, refusing his salvation, entrance into his kingdom, he looked down upon us, the dying, saying, "Father, forgive." Extravagantly merciful, even to his last breath (Luke 23:34). Jesus, good neighbor of all good neighbors.

Don't soften the shock, the outrage, that the unexpected (maybe even unwanted) hero of the story is a Samaritan. As John's Gospel explains, "Jews don't mess with Samaritans," or words to that effect (see John 4:9). Once, when Jesus's critics cursed him, they said, "You are a Samaritan and have a demon" (John 8:48).

The good neighbor to the man dying in the ditch is _____? A religious terrorist? A neo-Nazi? The rich guy who lives next door who posted an offensive yard sign and voted differently from you in the last election? Feel free to fill in the blank with your despised Samaritan.

When Augustine preached this story, he said the Samaritan is Jesus, our unexpected, though true neighbor who reached out in mercy, bandaged our wounds, even made our wounds his own. It's more than an example story that exhorts us to better human behavior; it's a story about the saving work of the Christ.

Julian of Norwich interpreted the victim, dying in the ditch from his wounds, then resurrected out of the ditch by divine mercy, as Christ, the only one who ever found a way out of the grave, the pioneer who goes ahead of us from death to life (Hebrews 12:1-3).

Many people my age say, "I don't want to be a burden to my family" or "I don't want to be dependent on the charity of others in my old age." We thereby show that we have been baptized into the American myth of self-sufficiency and independence. We fear being so in need that we'll need a neighbor.

Martin Luther King Jr. (who preached more sermons from Jesus's parables than any other genre of scripture) stressed the ethical imperative in the story. In one sermon King said that the lawyer and the Levite reminded him of most white preachers who are "more cautious than courageous" in their reluctance "to speak up for those in need." In a couple of sermons King asserted that the Black church had been sent down the dangerous Jericho road to rescue the sick-unto-death white church from its racist sins, to bind up its self-inflicted wounds and restore it to health.

King had the gall to tell an African American congregation that, in spite of all the wounds they had suffered from white supremacy sin, they were called by Jesus to be saviors of those who despised them.

"What must I do to earn my eternal life?" asks the lawyer. I'm a fairly well-fixed person of means. I want to be a good citizen. An afternoon a week tutoring disadvantaged youth? Ten percent off the top for charity? A pint of blood a month to the Red Cross? To whom must I be a neighbor in order to win myself a place in God's eternal kingdom?

At the story's ending, Jesus has turned the tables on his questioner. Not, to whom must I be a neighbor? But rather, "*Who has recklessly, extravagantly been a neighbor to me?*"

Maybe I'm more the good-as-dead, helpless, needy guy down in the ditch than I like to admit, in need of some Samaritan who doesn't mind getting down and dirty with the likes of me.

"What was your biggest challenge in AA?" I asked a recovering alcoholic.

He replied, "Having to admit that I couldn't save myself without help from somebody I can't stand."

Mother Mary had sung a song of mercy before Jesus's birth:

> *He shows mercy to everyone, . . .*
> *He has shown strength with his arm.*
> *He has scattered those with arrogant thoughts and proud*
> *inclinations.*
> *He has pulled the powerful down from their thrones*
> *and lifted up the lowly.*
> *He has filled the hungry with good things*
> *and sent the rich away empty-handed.*
> *He has come to the aid of his servant Israel,*
> *remembering his mercy,*
> *just as he promised to our ancestors,*
> *to Abraham and to Abraham's descendants forever.*
> (*Luke 1:50-55*)

Not much mercifulness out there at the moment. Ours shall not be known as the Age of Mercy. I listen to the news every day, waiting for our current leaders to use the five-letter word Jesus loved; they don't.

Just heard a podcaster rant that all of America's problems are due to "the sin of empathy." Empathetic thinking (which he said particularly afflicts women) leads government decision makers to make excuses for the irresponsibility of others, to rescue people from their own mistakes through empathetic social programs, and coddles people who ought to be punished rather than pitied.

Thank God the man never mentioned the one who, in his last meal, responded to our hunger with "This is my body, my blood, given [mercifully] for you."

Amid the famine of mercy, what a grand opportunity for Christians to rediscover the oddness of the King on a donkey who preached, "Happy are people who show mercy, because they will receive mercy" (Matthew 5:7).

Scripture has little to say about humanity's search for God; from start to finish the Bible is a long story of God's unrelenting, resourceful, determined search for us. We are not able to initiate or to sustain conversation with God; everything about our relationship with God begins and continues with God in Christ slinging seed our way, stooping down to bind up our wounds, with God's merciful resolve to be for us and for us to be with God.

The Samaritan not only stopped on his journey but also risked reaching out to the one in need in the ditch. That's good news: your relationship with God is at God's initiative. In Jesus Christ, God has mercifully taken responsibility for your connection with God.

It's all well and good that you are reading a book on the Last Supper. I hope that in reading you'll find yourself drawn closer to Christ.

Just remember that your reading this book was Christ's idea before it was yours. If you feel Jesus speaking to you from the words on this page, it's his revelation, his gift, grace, rather than your personal achievement. He doesn't wait for us to come to him; he makes the first move to us.

God's kingdom comes to us, not we to the Kingdom. The Kingdom's outbreak among us is God's doing, not the result of our good work, sincere believing, social activism, or reading books about the Kingdom.

You can rest secure in that. We don't have to climb up to God; in Jesus Christ, God descends, condescends to us. If we're to be rescued, saved, plucked out of whatever ditch we're in, it will be at the Lord's initiative:

> *Rescue comes from the LORD!*
> *May your blessing be on your people!*
> (Psalm 3:8)

So when Jesus says "Go and do likewise," maybe he's saying "This is who I am and what I'm up to. Now that you know that, why don't you join with me in my work in my world?" Go and do as Jesus goes and does.

"Go and do likewise" suggests that this parable has missional intent. God has elected the church to embody God's gracious intentions beyond the bounds of the church. We can't be faithful just hanging around the church; we've got to be out and about on the road. We are missionaries of a merciful Christ, looking for those who need mercy in the worst sort of way.

Others may be enemies of our country, or adversaries of the American way; God is not their enemy. Others may be undocumented to be citizens of the USA, but all are naturalized citizens of God's kingdom. If the church condemns the lifestyle of a group of people, the sinfulness of another culture, or the foreign policy of some hostile nation, we are under divine compulsion to make clear that God has elected them to be our sisters and brothers by electing *all* for God's salvation (1 Timothy 1:3-4). Mercy trumps condemnation when the church turns from talking about Jesus to talk with fellow sinners about sin in the name of a Savior who saves only sinners. How? Through the missionary endeavor of sinners partnering with God's merciful saving of fellow sinners.

As Mary Gauthier puts it in "Mercy Now," we find ourselves loving institutions—church and country—that have fallen into destructive patterns, yet recognizing that condemnation isn't the final word. Her song gives voice to the broader truth that "every single one of us could use some mercy now"—a mercy that doesn't calculate worthiness or wait for reform before extending itself. [3]

"Sure, we ought to love everybody, and though I don't want to see us turn anybody away from our church, I just don't think it's biblical to affirm people with those lifestyles. Love the sinner; hate the sin. Right? There are churches that don't see anything wrong with LGBTQ identities; let those congregations help them."

Countered a fellow church member, "My point was not that we ought to try to be a good neighbor to help them, but rather, maybe they could help us to be a more faithful church. We need them to be our good neighbors more then they need us."

Having grown up in South Carolina, during the days of legally enforced racial segregation, I'm grateful that, in my youth, a number of courageous, caring, reckless Black Christians were merciful good Samaritans to me. Witnessing to me, correcting me, telling the truth to me even when I didn't want to hear it so that I was saved, lifted out of the ditch of white racism where I lay dying, even though I didn't even know I was sick.

After an evening at table at Martha and Mary's place, Jesus and his comrades resume their journey (Luke 10:38-42). And we all know where that walk will end, and how we shall repay the Sower, the Samaritan for such extravagant, reckless, risky mercy.

Chapter 2
OPEN
INVITATION

On his way to the Last Supper, Jesus careens from one dinner party to the next (in Luke's Gospel, ten of them) turning a dining room into a classroom (Luke 5:27-39; 7:36-50; 9:10-17; 10:38-42; 11:37-54; 14:1-24; 19:1-10; 22:7-38; 24:13-35; and 24:36-53), all culminating in a Thursday Passover supper where Jesus will take a loaf of bread, a cup of wine, and pronounce, "This is my body, given for you. . . . This is my blood shed for you . . ." (Luke 22:19-20).

One Sabbath, a Pharisee invited Jesus to his house to share a sacred Sabbath meal (Luke 14:1-24). "They were watching him closely" (Greek: *paratēroumenoi*) (Luke 14:1). And so are we. Having seen Jesus wreak havoc at Simon's table, we doubt that things will go well for host, guests, or us.

And they don't. "Trouble" is Jesus's middle name.

Before the hors d'oeuvres are served, a sad, suffering, sick man barges in seeking healing from Jesus. (What is it about Jesus that attracts unexpected table companions?) Jesus makes the dinner table into a hospital gurney. Push aside the plates, crystal, and silverware. Upsy-daisy. "Let's see what we can do for this poor guy. 'Abnormal body swelling'?" shouts Jesus, medical confidentiality be damned. "I'll have you better in no time."

Excursus: In a previous meal, a "woman of the city" intruded into a meal. Now, it's a suffering sick man. In both cases, Jesus uses their incursions to tell some of his best stories, to expand people's notions about who God is and what God's up to. Here's a question: Anybody showing up at your church's table times uninvited, even unwanted who may be sent there by God to expand your congregation's notions of how to be the body of Christ? Discuss amongst yourselves.

Of course, the host is mortified by this intruder and by Jesus's response. Assorted, "Well, I never . . . ," and "How dare he? On the Sabbath!" from the guests.

Jesus heals the man, helps him back on his feet, and tells him to go, get on with the rest of his life. Get it? Jesus's healings are hors d'oeuvres, a foretaste of the main course when God's kingdom comes and all shall sing, "Look! God's dwelling is here with humankind. . . . He will wipe away every tear from their eyes. . . . There will be no mourning, crying, or pain anymore, for the former things have passed away" (Revelation 21:3-4).

But Jesus is better even than a doctor. As if miraculously healing a sick person were not enough, Jesus seizes the opportunity to pick a food fight.

As the lawyers and Pharisees at the table give Jesus the old *paratēroumenoi*, Jesus asks, "I know it's not right to work on the Sabbath, but is it okay to do good work?"

Awkward silence.

"Can't heeeear you." Another riddle: "Say for instance your child or favorite ox [odd coupling, that one] chose the Sabbath to fall into a ditch. Wouldn't you pull it out?"

Again, silence all round the table. Maybe "ditch" evokes uncomfortable memories of the story Jesus told about the Samaritan. The Pharisee senses that the meal is careening out of his control. Another Sabbath meal trashed by Jesus.

With that, Jesus once again turns on his fellow guests. Noting how they jockey for "the best seats at the table," he tells them a story.

When someone invites you to a party, don't take the best seat at the table, otherwise you'll be embarrassed when a more eminent guest arrives. And you're mortified by being ousted to a less prominent place at the table. It's better to be invited to step up than to be forced to move down.

"All who lift themselves up will be brought low, and those who make themselves low will be lifted up" (Luke 14:11).

After a fun round of Get the Guests, Jesus (as usual) smacks his host: "And as for you, next time you give one of these stuffed-shirt, deadly dull wakes you call a dinner party, don't invite your buddies at the club, the few family members who still speak to you, or your fat-cat neighbors (death to any party). All they'll do is to pay you back with another boring evening at Pebble Beach. What fun is that? Instead, when you give a banquet, invite the poor, crippled, lame, and blind; they'll never repay" (Luke 14:13).

"These forgotten and marginalized, who never get invited into this part of town, and need a good meal in the worst way, can never repay you; you'll be repaid for more than the meal costs you when it comes to the greatest party of all, the Great Banquet at the Resurrection."

Jesus is not telling riddles, puzzles that are tough to figure out; he is giving direct instruction on how to live your way into the practical ethics of the Kingdom that's breaking out among us here, now.

Take heart. Jesus is not calling upon you to be a spiritual hero, casting your body to the lions. He's inviting you to be part of the Kingdom where the bar is always open, the wine is free, the table is large, the door is forever ajar, and the expansive gaggle of guests looks like Jesus's idea of a good time.

It was 5:45 p.m. I was dog-tired after a wearisome day doing work for God's Kingdom Inc., otherwise known as Northside United Methodist Church. Finally locking the church door, I was at last ready to make my weary way home. My heart sank when I saw shuffling toward me on the church sidewalk a disheveled-looking man.

Just my luck, some guy down on his luck wanting a handout. I'll head him off here at the door, give him a twenty, and head home. No time and not in the mood for somebody's sad story.

"Are you the preacher?" he asked before I could get the jump on him.

"Yes," I said glumly. "Locking up. Heading home. I guess you're here for a handout."

He began, "Well, you see, I was . . ."

"No need. Here, twenty-five is all I've got. Hope this helps," I said, without the slightest trace of graciousness.

He took the cash, stared at it for a moment, then stuffed it in his soiled trousers. "I suppose you expect me to thank you," said he, with surprising snideness. "So you can feel good about yourself."

"Some show of gratitude wouldn't hurt," said I, annoyed.

"Well, I ain't goin' to thank you 'cause I know you were forced to help me whether you wanted to or not. He" (now pointing upward toward the cross on top of our church) "made you do it. Didn't ask you how you feel about it. He didn't give you no choice in helping a hungry soul, did he?"

Just then Luke 14:13, came to mind.

Amid the uncomfortable, maybe even angry silence around the Pharisee's table that followed Jesus's instruction on table etiquette, at hearing mention of the future Resurrection feast, one of the guests blurts a pious jingle: "Happy are those who will feast in God's kingdom" (Luke 14:15).

The guest's sappy comment reminds Jesus of another feast story (Luke 14:16-24): "A certain man hosted a large dinner and invited many people. When it was time for the dinner to begin, he sent his servant to tell the invited guests, 'Come! The dinner is now ready.'"

The response of the invitees to the biggest bash this town has ever seen?

"One by one, they all began to make excuses. The first one told him, 'I bought a farm and must go and see it. Please excuse me.' Another said, 'I bought five teams of oxen, and I'm going to check on them. Please excuse me.' Another said, 'I just got married, so I can't come.'"

In a region where arable land is scarce, this guy has bought a farm and hasn't seen it? A farmer purchased costly farm animals before checking them out? A patriarchal Near Eastern male lets a wife keep him from a huge banquet with his buddies?

Everybody is rolling under the table in laughter at the absurdity, the insult of these excuses.

Or maybe, depending on your personality, these are good excuses. Is providing for the well-being of your family not a good thing? Taking care of business is what businesspeople are supposed to do. Don't we believe that sacrificing your social life for your marriage and family is a great virtue? "I'd do anything for my family," we brag—even beg out of an invitation to a feast.

But the caterers have been paid, the table is set, and the "certain man" is determined to party. Whether the excuses are frivolous or virtuous, "The master of the house became angry and said to his servant, 'Go quickly to the city's streets, the busy ones and the side streets, and bring the poor, crippled, blind, and lame'" (Luke 14:21).

Get it? God's kingdom coming is a banquet with a bunch of people with whom we wouldn't be caught dead on a Saturday night. Since we're all, every single one of us, on our way to being mortified anyway, why not get over our stuffy, self-righteous I'd-rather-die-than-dine-with-the-likes-of-you standoffishness and come to God's party?

God's kingdom is a big bash in which the poor, crippled, blind, and lame, who are excluded from the official celebrations in our kingdoms, are now invited—no, eagerly sought out guests at God's table.

In the parable of the Sower, we were told that the biggest impediments to discipleship were possessions, family, and cares of the world. This parable implies that the lack of all this baggage is a grand opportunity for evangelism. Those who, in their hunger and need, are free on a Saturday night, desperate for healing and mercy, and more open to a dinnertime invitation are advantaged in the topsy-turvy world of God's kingdom. They are more likely to say yes to the feast of a lifetime.

As a campus minister, I remember seeing a list of "Students who are most open to an evangelistic appeal." Right under "Students who suffer from chronic depression" and "Students who feel out of place at the university" were "Students whose parents have gone through a terrible divorce." In other words, the main requirement for being at this grand table is to be honest-to-God hungry hearted.

My favorite worship moment at the Lord's Supper on Maundy Thursday is when, at my invitation to Communion, the congregation comes forward and holds out their hands for the bread and wine.

Many of those who come to the table are privileged and powerful. But as they hold out their hands, the preacher in me wants to say "Look. Your hands are empty. You seem to need a gift. Grace."

What's normal, natural, all-American is for our hands to grab, grip, and hold on tight to whatever stuff we can snatch. What we must be taught by the church is the unnatural gesture of holding out empty, open hands, honestly admitting we need a gracious God to give us what we can't earn for ourselves.

"Our biggest challenge as a church is that most of our folks have second homes at the beach or the mountains," complained a pastor. Limit your guest list to one economic bracket, expect lots of empty seats at the table.

In his Sermon on the Plain, Jesus proclaimed God's kingdom as a great topsy-turvy reversal, promising,

> *Happy are you who are poor,*
> > *because God's kingdom is yours.*
> *Happy are you who hunger now,*
> > *because you will be satisfied.*
> *Happy are you who weep now,*
> > *because you will laugh.*
> > > *(Luke 6:20-21)*

But as for the well-heeled:

> *But how terrible for you who are rich,*
> > *because you have already received your comfort.*
> *How terrible for you who have plenty now,*
> > *because you will be hungry.*
> *How terrible for you who laugh now,*
> > *because you will mourn and weep.*
> > > *(Luke 6:24-25)*

Tears for those who have experienced this world as good as it gets, laughter later for those for whom the world's kingdoms have meant misery.

The poor are invited, not because they are, after all, once you get to know them, good people a lot like us. God graciously invites all. When we who are rich, over-comforted, over-blessed, and happy refuse, God gladly goes to those who have no hope for a good meal but God.

Here's a supper prepared, not for the first twelve to show up, but by a host "who wants all people to be saved and to come to a knowledge of the truth" (1 Timothy 2:4). All.

The poor are not invited in the hope that, if the poor could just get a good break, they'd pull themselves up by their bootstraps, learn to fend for themselves, buy a minivan, and become middle-class taxpayers. (Give a man a fish, he'll be hungry tomorrow, teach a man to fish . . . and all that.) Those in need are invited, as are we all, not because of who they are or aspire to be, but because of who God is. The poor, crippled, blind, and lame shall feast at the kingdom table because, like Jesus repeatedly told us, this is who God is and the good that God is up to, lifting up the lowly, depressing the proud, feeding the hungry, disappointing the well-filled.

We, the rich, are notorious for our excuses: "I'm not all that well off," "Getting harder every day to put bread on the table," "There's a lot of welfare fraud and waste. Offer 'em a job and, if they don't take it, let 'em starve."

The too-proud-to-get-down-and-party excuse-makers exclude themselves from the banquet. Have fun all by yourself, stuck at home on a Friday night, whooping it up watching reruns of *The Bachelor*. You have nobody to blame but yourself.

I remind you that this string of table time stories began when one of the guests mouthed the platitude, "Oh how fortunate we'll be one day, someday, in that select company who eat heavenly bread in God's kingdom" (Luke 14:15).

After a nasty church fight in one of my early congregations, when tempers had cooled, one of our matriarchs pronounced, "We might as well start learning how to get along with one another here; it would be just like the Lord to seat us next to one another for eternity."

Paul tells his early congregations that God is now doing in their churches that which will be done everywhere and for eternity when God's kingdom fully comes. The invited have nothing to offer, little to commend their being seated at so grand an affair. Everything is in the invitation. Look at us, says Paul to one of his sorriest of churches, "God chose what the world considers low-class and low-life—[we nobodies]—to reduce what is considered to be something to nothing" (1 Corinthians 1:28).

Your congregation—the first act of the great upheaval God means to work on our whole society, a showcase for the vast regime change in which those who've been blessed by every invitation to come up, are being cast down by their proud refusal to let down their hair and party.

Even before Jesus was born, Mother Mary predicted as much in her Advent hymn:

> *He has pulled the powerful down from their thrones*
> *and lifted up the lowly.*
> *He has filled the hungry with good things*
> *and sent the rich away empty-handed.*
> (Luke 1:52-53)

So if you still think that Jesus is here to help you adjust and fit more comfortably into ways of the kingdoms of this world, then you haven't been listening.

One of Jesus's favorite words in Luke's Gospel and in Acts is *today*. He opened his inaugural sermon at his hometown synagogue in Nazareth with "today." After reading from the Isaiah scroll, he announced, "Today, this scripture has been fulfilled just as you heard it" (Luke 4:21). The kingdom of heaven, not just a wishful hope someday, one day, maybe. It's kingdom now. Today.

Scholars wonder if Luke's Gospel is meant to reassure early Christians who were disappointed by Christ's delayed return. Jesus says he's coming soon, but here we are, listening to Luke listen to Jesus, maybe a century after Christ's cross, resurrection, and ascension, and he ain't returned yet. What's a believer to do in the meantime? Sure, thy kingdom come, thy will be done—but *when*?

When speculation about the date and time for the arrival of the Kingdom reached a fever pitch, Jesus, in exasperation, said, "God's kingdom is already among you" (Luke 17:21).

Here? Jesus, where? When?

Yes. Right here, right now. In his parables, most of them based in familiar, ordinary, daily life, Jesus contemporizes the kingdom of God. As if to say, "Want to know why I'm telling you all these stories and tossing out these riddles? Open your eyes! See the kingdom breaking out right here, now, among you! There's no need to sit around thinking about heaven someday, one day. Heaven's kingdom is here, now."

In Jesus's parable of the Great Banquet, the invitation isn't just to some future heavenly feast, it's also to a meal that's in session this very moment, if we just have the eyes to see the bit of bread and the sip of wine we're given on Maundy Thursday as foretaste, hors d'oeuvres before the banquet that never ends. Where is God's kingdom? It's wherever, whenever the maimed, the blind, and the lame are invited to the table. Want to see God? Look around at that motley crew gathered with you at the Lord's Table on Holy Thursday evening, Christ's idea of a good time. We're doing here, now, in church that which we shall one day do for eternity.

The parable of the Great Banquet is true. God's party is in swing this week, at your church and mine, "He has [here, now] filled the hungry with good things / and sent the rich away empty-handed" (Luke 1:53).

That's why the mark of your church (your local rendition of Jesus's table fellowship) is not only how many of the hungry your church feeds but also how many of the hungry join you at the Lord's Table. Christ isn't waiting to show up at the end; open your eyes, he's here. Now.

Don't waste your time looking for kingdom outbreak on the floor of the US Senate, or at the Pentagon, much less at a state dinner at the White House. Look local: your kitchen table that you've opened to someone who didn't think they belonged, potluck suppers in the church basement for people who had never set foot in a church, at the Lord's Table next Sunday.

Whenever there's Jesus-like hospitality, graciousness, and openhanded invitation, surprise! We are on hand, for the kingdom of mercy that is at hand. "Happy are those who will feast in God's kingdom" (Luke 14:15) indeed.

You can't aspire to be at the table or work hard to earn a seat at the feast; you can only be invited, the same way the disciples gathered with Jesus at the Last Supper. Your parentage, intelligence, race, status, gender, education, even belief count for little with the Lord of the banquet. If you're in a church this Sunday, heck, if you are reading this book, getting anything out of it, feeling closer to God because of it, it's only at God's open invitation.

Doubts? Bad church experience in the past? Don't know Genesis from Jeremiah? Burdened by past screwups? Come to the feast. Have some bread. Take some wine. This feast is for you. We boast no other merit to be at that table other than "I've been invited."

Listen to us trying to take credit for our being at the Lord's Table: "Since I've accepted Jesus as my Savior," "Now that I've taken Jesus into my heart." Or "Since I gave my life to Christ." Note the preponderance of the first-person singular. That may play into the American self-help, mother-I'd-rather-do-it-myself story but clashes with Jesus's stories of his open invitation.

If you've never been excluded from a party, rented a tux only to find that your invitation got lost in the mail, been turned away at the door because your name is not on the list, or on the other hand, if you've never been surprised by an invitation to the biggest bash this town's ever seen, even when you didn't expect to make the cut, then I'm unsure if I'm a good enough preacher to explain this parable to you. Still, I'll try, on the conviction that Jesus will open your eyes to the good news: *You're included.*

Though the host is angry (and sad, too, we suspect) that the invitation has been refused, and though there's lots of judgment to go around, there's no support here for excluding anyone from the Lord's Table. If there's judgment, it's for those who are supposed to be hosts, not for the suitability of the guests. Jesus doesn't allow us to choose whom he'll entertain at his board. We know the center of God's kingdom—Christ—but nobody has ever discovered its circumference boundaries. Open table.

Jesus was sent to a cross for receiving, inviting, eating, and drinking with sinners, some of whom are religious experts whose sin is in their vaunted knowledge of Sabbath keeping and all matters biblical, others are just your garden-variety sinners: women of the city, the sick and the maimed, everybody around the table who is uncomfortable with Jesus's reckless guest list, Pharisees and tax collectors, the poor and the heretofore uninvited. In other words, the same crowd who gathered with him at the Last Supper. And just about everybody reading this book.

He welcomes to his Table not only the poor and the dispossessed but also his most vocal enemies. He sups even with his watchful pharisaical critics, though as we have seen, it could be the most uncomfortable meal of their lives.

You'd think that would be the end of the story: Let the banquet begin. Too bad about the "empty-handed" ones who missed the feast. But Jesus is on a roll and so he adds one more twist to the tale, the punchline to this joke that's on us: "The servant said, 'Master, your instructions have been followed and there is still room.' The master said to the servant, 'Go to the highways and back alleys and urge people to come in so that my house will be filled'" (Luke 14:22-23).

I want you to take "there is still room" as the key to this Big Banquet riddle.

The lord of the banquet doesn't stop inviting after the first wave of refusals or even the second group of acceptances. At this expansive table, there's still room. Don't just post on Facebook that there's still room, "Go," "urge," actively seek and search for those who haven't gotten the news: You're included. "There's still room."

Didn't grow up in a Christian home? Parents spent their lives rebelling against their fundamentalist Christian upbringing and didn't worry about your faith development? Messed up bad when you were in your twenties? Fell in with the wrong crowd at work? No reservation? No problem. We can easily squeeze you in. There's a place that's set just for you. No excuse is good, nobody's refusal is accepted, and anybody's no is not the last word.

The host has been laboring in the hot kitchen for days and won't rest until everybody in town is at the table. The party comes, not through the invitees' hard work, upright living, or social justice efforts for a utopian society. It's all due to the gracious, invitational efforts of the Sower, the Savior, the Host who sends out emissaries with the news "There's still room!"

"Salvation for all!" cried out John Wesley in the fields and alleyways of England, obedient to Christ's command, "Go to the highways and back alleys and urge people to come in so that my house will be filled" (Luke 14:23).

All of us are here at the Lord's Table as living, bodily, visible proof that we've got a gracious God who won't take no for an answer.

Early on in his ministry, when the people of Capernaum wanted him to linger awhile in their town, Jesus refused to slow down and settle in, so intent was he to deliver the invitation: "I must preach the good news of God's kingdom in other cities too, for this is why I was sent" (Luke 4:43), ever the invitationalist who won't rest until there's a full house (Luke 14:23). On Thursday, at the Last Supper, Jesus will say to his disciples that he's been looking forward to this Passover meal since the beginning of the trip; relentless host all the way to the end (Luke 22:15).

That's your first, last, best hope, in life, in death, in any life beyond death: Your end, your eschaton, will be your beginning. After you've breathed your last, and everybody has left what's left of you at the cemetery, you'll hear those gracious words, "Good news; there's room for you."

As we continue our Lenten journey with Jesus to the cross, we'll see this story repeated, in one way or another: God's gracious invitation, humanity's rejection, followed by God's rejection of our rejection, God's inclusive yes to all, followed by our collective "No!" then God's resurrection rejection of our cruciform rejection. Because of who God is, namely, the one who told this story, there's still room.

Find some of Jesus's riddles insoluble? Don't get the point of his jokes? Worry not; there's still room. Having a good sense of humor is not a requirement for getting into this banquet; nobody's here except by invitation. And the invitation is given to all.

"Our church is a loving, caring family. If anybody in this congregation has a need, somebody has your back."

Sorry, not good enough. Any church that's not actively out on the "highways and back alleys" delivering the message ("Hey, there's still room.") is not yet fully a church.

The median age in my denomination is sixty-three (by the time you read this it will be at least sixty-four). What's wrong with this picture?

(BTW: When the exasperated host gives instructions to his servant to garner the second round of invitees, Jesus switches from second-person singular "you," to second-person plural, "you all" [Luke 14:24]. This is in no way a private party. In Jesus's evangelistic entourage, nobody is permitted to keep the good news to themselves, everybody is a messenger of the invitation: "There's still room!")

Anytime your church gets in gear and engages in mission, whenever a somnambulant congregation stirs into action in extroverted evangelism, you're only following the ongoing work of an out-and-about Master who keeps slinging seed, searching and seeking, relentlessly inviting, sending out servants into every corner of the world, proclaiming, "There's still room."

One reason why there's too little inviting is that many of us have been feasting at the Master's table for so long that we forget that we are there only by invitation. We get confused into thinking that we were born Christian, that following Jesus is normal, natural, American, by birthright. If you can't remember when you weren't a Christian, there's a good chance that you've forgotten the evangelist who gave you the invitation.

Take a moment and think back over your journey with Jesus. Who was it who found a way to get across to you the good news, "There's still room," in such a way that you knew that this banquet's for you?

The main reason people give for not trying out church: "Nobody ever invited me."

In Luke's memory of the parable of the Great Banquet, the stress is upon the relentless seeking and searching, the repeated invitations. Still, there's judgment. An invitation isn't accomplished until it's received. The judgment in the parable comes not from the Master: "Sorry. Full up. Reached our quota of the likes of you. The door is shut. Too bad that you got here after our fifteen-minute grace period for reservations. Your table is taken. Your name's not on the list."

No, if there's judgment in this parable, it's by self-recrimination: "I just stupidly turned down an invitation to the party of my life in order to spend more time culling my files at the office."

The parable ends with the gracious, relentlessly inviting host saying, maybe sadly, "I tell you, not one of those who were invited will taste my dinner" (Luke 14:24). The parable of joyful invitation to a banquet ends with sad judgment upon those who were originally invited but made excuses. Jesus himself wept over Jerusalem's refusal of his invitation (Luke 13:34). The Master stands, peering out the opened door into the night, hoping that the servants have succeeded in getting more guests to come to the table. There's still room.

At end of John's Gospel, three times the risen Christ asks Peter, "Simon, son of John, do you love me?" Jesus, ever the consummate host, says simply, "Feed my sheep" (John 21:17).

Lest we take Jesus's command too parochially, as if the invitation to the table extends no farther than the bounds of our congregation, Jesus says, "I have other sheep that don't belong to this sheep pen. I must lead them too. They will listen to my voice and there will be one flock, with one shepherd" (John 10:16). Is there no limit to Jesus's determination to seek, search, save until everybody is at his party?

I think you know the answer.

"My Father's house has room to spare," said Jesus (John 14:2). Even for a dying thief on a cross, even for a "woman of the city," a wandering lost sheep, even for smug, peering Pharisees, and know-it-all Bible experts beating everybody else over the head with God's word, even at the last for Jesus's twelve best friends who turned out to be Jesus's most disappointing betrayers, there's still room.

At our end, when there's a funeral, long, elaborate, prevaricating eulogies are beside the point. When we've breathed our last, our sole hope is to hear the words, "Come on in. We've been waiting for you. Take a seat, enjoy the party that never ends."

On Maundy Thursday, once we were all assembled at the table in the upper room, Jesus dropped the bombshell: "My betrayer is with me; his hand is on this table" (Luke 22:21). All of us took our grubby, guilty hands off the table as we asked, "Is it I Lord?" knowing that any of us could betray our Lord. Some even protested, "Although everybody may cut and run, I'll have your back!"

Snapshot of the first Eucharist at the very first church: Jesus sharing a meal surrounded by a bunch of lying, grumbling betrayers—who happen to be his very best friends for whom he's on his way to give his life.

At the table, sharing the meal, was Judas. Like everyone that night, Judas was there by invitation. Judas, the one who betrayed our Lord for money, and with a kiss, was among the first of the invitees.

I'm glad Judas was at the table. If Christ had not invited Judas to be there, how could I be here, shamelessly holding out my guilty, hungry, dirty, empty hands for the bread and wine, Christ's body and blood? I'm glad Judas was there, thankful that when I approached God's door it was opened to me, happy to have heard those blessed words, that even for me, as for Judas, "There's still room."

Chapter 3
FEASTING WITH THE FOUND

"All the tax collectors and sinners were gathering around Jesus to listen to him. The Pharisees and legal experts were grumbling, saying, 'This man welcomes sinners and eats with them'" (Luke 15:1-2).

The grumblers don't accuse Jesus of heresy or bad Bible interpretation. They grumble, "This charlatan can't be the Messiah; look at the riffraff with whom he dines!"

I know you'd like Jesus to respond, "But you see, I'm going to redeem this riffraff, teach 'em good manners, clean 'em up and polish them off so they'll be worthy of admission to the Great Messianic Banquet. Someday. One day. Whenever it finally comes."

No. Jesus answers his critics with some of his most memorable (and for many, maddening) mealtime riddles:

"Say, one of you shepherds has a hundred sheep. One wanders. Which of you would not desert the ninety-nine and go out and beat the bushes day and night until you find that one lost sheep?

"And when you finally find it, would you not call your friends and neighbors saying, 'Let's party! I found my lost sheep!'" (Luke 15:3-7).

(To which your neighbors reply, "Hey, genius. While you were away searching for one, most of the ninety-nine have bolted. Sure you want to celebrate?")

Remember that earlier sloppy Sower who lost so much good seed through reckless sowing? He switched jobs. Now he's trying his hand at animal husbandry where he's become the shepherd who risks a flock of ninety-nine good, stay-at-home (though uncreative and risk-averse) sheep to go search for a single wayward, willful, wandering lamb.

Which one of you wouldn't do that?

People are rolling in the aisles with laughter. "Tell us another one, Jesus," they hoot.

"Or what woman among you, owning ten coins, loses one? So of course you tear up the house, move the heavy appliances out on the porch, toss the sofa onto the front yard, rip out the carpet and once you find that lost coin, you run into the street, screaming to your neighbors, 'I found my penny! I'm blowing every dime I've got to throw the biggest banquet this town's ever seen. You're all invited. Come as you are'" (Luke 15:8-10).

Now, which one of you wouldn't do that?

Nobody would act like that. None of us would engage in such horrible home economics or scandalous shepherding, much less throw an expensive party for a trifle like one recovered sheep or a single small coin retrieved. None of us.

These are not stories about us. *These are stories about God.* God is not a cosmic bureaucrat, with nine-to-five office hours, treating everybody the same, doing a cost-benefit analysis and acting prudently in accord with sound business practices. God is the recklessly seeking shepherd, the woman furiously searching until she finds what was lost. God's kingdom accounting is different from what counts in our kingdoms.

Though I was a child when I heard it, I still remember our pastor's sermon, "The Most Wonderful, Comforting Word in the Bible." The word? It's prominent in these two stories: *until.*

When does a recklessly seeking God call off the hunt for the lost, give up hope for the harvest, cease searching for the strays, rescind the invitation to the feast?

When a person blasphemes, "I'll be damned if I believe that Jesus Christ is Lord"? When someone dies without having accepted God's invitation? If a miscreant commits an act so irredeemably horrible that no amount of repenting makes up for what they've done, aren't they beyond retrieval? Hitler? Stalin?

All we know for sure are stories of a relentlessly searching shepherd and a determinedly seeking woman who searched and sought *until . . .*

Now Jesus's comic set moves into one of the most outrageous God's kingdom jokes of all. "Which one of you fathers, having two sons, and the younger says, 'Dad, I've had enough of this hick town. Drop dead. Put the will into effect and give me my share of your estate.' Now which one of you daddies would not do just that?"

The father gives the upstart, impudent, demanding younger brother the keys to the Rolls, the code to the family safe, stock portfolio, and deeds to half of all the family property. Without so much as a "Thanks, Dad," the ungrateful little wretch kicks up gravel in the driveway as he heads out for the high life in the big city in the far country.

There he rebelliously engaged in, as the Common English Bible euphemistically calls it, "extravagant living" (Luke 5:13). Though Jesus doesn't specify, feel free to let your salacious imagination run loose and supply whatever forms of "extravagant living" you find particularly repugnant (when engaged in by other people).

In a short time, the kid has blown through the whole wad. He became enslaved to a prominent pig farmer (about as low as you can go for a kosher-keeping Jew), so hungry he would gladly have supped on pig slop.

Then, in an evocative phrase, Jesus says "he came to his senses," saying, "Wait a minute. I've got a father, a home."

On his way homeward, barefoot and in rags, he begins to compose a penitent speech: "Dad, I mean, Father. (Woe is me.) I have sinned against heaven and against you. (Beats chest three times.) I no longer deserve to be called your son. (Weep, wail, gnash teeth for good effect.) Take me on as one of your hired hands." (I deserve no better for my stupidity.) "What's on for supper?" (Luke 15:18-19).

"While he was still a long way off, his father saw him and was moved with compassion. His father ran to him, hugged him, and kissed him" (Luke 15:20). Not waiting for the son to come groveling back, the father goes out to meet his son.

The son begins his remorseful speech, "Father, I have sinned against heaven and you . . ."

Turns out that the father doesn't give a rip for contrite speeches. "Save the Repentance Drama for your application to Law School. You wanted a party? I'll show you a party. Bring out the best robe and put it on him! You lusted for an extravagant lifestyle? I'll show you prodigality. Put a ring on his finger and Guccis on his feet! Fetch the fattened calf! Let the party begin!"

The father interrupts his son's planned penitent speech. He treats him, not as a repentant servant but as a son, no, as an honored guest at a profuse party, treating him, not like the little wretch he is, but like a king: best robe, ring, and fancy sandals.

Then poignantly the father says, "This son of mine was dead and has come back to life! He was lost and is found!" And the party begins.

Which one of you parents would not do that?

I'll answer for all of us: No sane, responsible parent would do that. You treat that kind of kid like a king, he'll think that his prodigality is appropriate. He'll make a habit of dissing his elders, wasteful extravagance, and end up living in a van down by the river.

Not a parent here who would pass up the opportunity to give a scolding lecture rather than an extravagant party, so eager would we be to leverage the rare, "Dad, I'm sorry" into an occasion to assert parental moral authority and control. Instead, all the father says is a joyful shout to the world, "We must celebrate with feasting because this son of mine was dead and has come back to life! He was lost and is found!" (Luke 15:23-24).

The expression "They began to celebrate" (make merry, party, get down, whoop it up) is repeated in a succession of merrymaking in Luke: 15:24, 29, 32 also 12:19 and 16:19. Earthly grumbling at Jesus's outrageous lack of dinnertime decorum evokes three parables in a row about heavenly joy. No sadness at lostness, no seriousness about sin overcomes the insistence upon heaven's rejoicing. God is determined to throw a never-ending party, and God will be darned if our bad choices will stifle the celebration.

What we wanted was for the father to receive the boy back home. Heck, we would have done that. Then there's supposed to be an unsmiling lecture filling the air with talk of "responsibility," "maturity," and "morality" followed by, "Alright, Howard. You've seen the error of your ways. You are forgiven since you have sincerely confessed to the mess you've made of things. Let this day be the first day of responsible adulthood and good citizenship. Why don't you shave, shower, and we'll give you a good, well-balanced, nourishing, gluten-free meal. Then we'll talk about removing that nose ring and completing your application to law school."

What we get is the father's extravagant (might I say, wasteful, prodigal) unconditional party to welcome back a profligate.

I recall a guest preacher in Duke Chapel giving a fine account of the reception of the prodigal son and the father's party. Then, as if suddenly realizing that she was preaching to a university congregation, said, "Now you young people, you students, should not take the father's graciousness as license for irresponsible behavior, the abuse of chemical substances, poor sleep habits, or neglecting your studies."

All good advice that's applauded by every parent in the congregation. Unfortunately for us preacherly and parental scolds, Jesus says none of that. He ends simply, "And they began to boogey!"

The scandal is not that the father welcomed back the wayward son; which one of us would not have done the same? Most of the details in the parable describe the over-the-top party. It's the party that gets us.

The party doesn't sit well with the older brother, either.

The music changes from Pearl Jam to Pachelbel. Enter the Dean of Students, the head of the Christian Family Coalition, and the Assistant Principal at your Junior High escorting in their favorite character, the Older Brother.

> Now his older son was in the field. Coming in from the field, he approached the house and heard music and dancing. He called one of the servants and asked what was going on. The servant replied, "Your brother has arrived, and your father has slaughtered the fattened calf because he received his son back safe and sound." Then the older son was furious and didn't want to enter . . .
>
> (Luke 15:25-28)

Nostrils flared, look of righteous indignation, "A party? And on a Wednesday! Listen you [not the most respectful way to address Dad], all this expense for an over-the-top vulgarly extravagant bash just because this son of yours" (Hear the sarcasm?) "staggers back home after blowing all your money on whores." (Excuse me. Jesus never mentioned "whores." All Jesus said was that the prodigal son lived "extravagantly." Maybe that meant that he ate high-fructose snacks. How quickly the rage of the righteous at the generosity of the father for "this child of yours" degenerates into angry accusations of debauchery, injustice, stock market manipulation, influence peddling, corruption, i.e., "whores.")

The older brother's grumbling reminds us of the griping of the Pharisees that occasioned this parable. We got here first. We've sat through years of boring Bible studies and engaged in Lenten self-denial practices, not to say a hundred Sundays of deadly dull sermons. And yet, when at last this little wayward lamb staggers in, smelling of booze and the cheap perfume of harlots, he gets a standing ovation? Is this any way to run the world?

"All this time I have served you, turning your sadly outdated farm into a profitable venture and never once did you throw a celebration for me and my friends" (we suspect his friends are few) "but when this son of yours shows up, you waste all that I've worked so hard to achieve on a ridiculously expensive party."

"Son, all that I have is yours," responds the father. "When this brother of yours" (hear the compassion?) "who was as good as dead" (note the deep sense of loss) "is brought back to life" (an Easter allusion?) "we just had to celebrate."

The older brother, expert on propriety, upholder of morality, refused to come in and join the party. The story ends with the sound of raucous music and dirty dancing inside, but with the father outside, in the dark, pleading with the brother to shuck his moral superiority complex, come in, and get down and party.

The elder brother is a "good person," in the worst sense of the word. Some of us are either the younger brother or the elder, depending on how we react to God's amazing grace. Grace for me is good but when it's grace for you, considering how suspect your repentance is when compared with mine, then sometimes grace doesn't feel so amazing.

As bishop I sent a pastor to a sad, dwindling little church. "First Sunday," she reported, "only eight people there. Eight! I despaired.

"'All the young people have moved out of the county,' they told me.

"But I noticed, in the piney woods beyond the train tracks, there were shacks with people living in them. Children too; lots of kids. So I went out there and told them, 'I'll pick you up on Sunday, take you to church, preach you a sermon, and then give you a big dinner afterward.'

"That Sunday, ten new folks came to church and dinner. In three weeks, I baptized four of them."

"Wow," said I. "Hilda, you get this year's Evangelism Award. Way to go."

"Not so fast, bishop. I baptized four but lost five of my church members, some of them were tithers too."

"You baptized four and lost five?" I asked.

"They said, on their way out, 'We don't want to go to church with a bunch of crackheads and their kids.'"

The elder brother's refusal of the feast shows that just because you've never been to the far country or engaged in debauched, I mean, "extravagant" living (whores and all) you can still be lost, standing stubbornly out in the dark as the party begins. Just the sort of older sibling who would write a book about Maundy

Thursday for fellow older siblings who are more comfortable discussing Lenten books in the church parlor than partying on Bourbon Street at Mardi Gras.

Take my first church in rural Georgia. Please. Fisticuffs in the parking lot after a trustee meeting that went bad. Adultery post-Wednesday night choir practice. Two weeks failing to receive my one hundred dollar a week salary due to the busted budget.

"Where is your church?" fellow Emory grad students would ask. "Thirty miles up Interstate 85 and two hundred years from Atlanta," I'd glumly reply.

One day I poured out my heart to a beloved professor. The failed fall stewardship campaign, the fights, the adultery. Oh yes, and the hound that somebody let in who ate the communion bread right off the altar. They thought it was funny.

My professor listened sympathetically, charitably outraged that someone of my talent and ability (graduate of Yale Divinity School) stuck out there with people like them. Then he sighed, but with a twinkle in his eye, said, "Worst of all, Jesus says those whores and tax collectors get to go into the kingdom before us good ones."

I have met the grumbling, stuffy older brother: me.

Proof text: "Jesus said to them, I assure you that tax collectors and prostitutes are entering God's kingdom ahead of you. For John came to you on the righteous road, and you didn't believe him. But tax collectors and prostitutes believed him. Yet even after you saw this, you didn't change your hearts and lives and you didn't believe him," and join God's Kingdom Party (Matthew 21:31-32).

Please note that the parable does not claim that the father loved one son more than the other. Neither son is rejected or judged; both are chosen and loved by a father who gives to both all that he's got. The younger son screws up and gets a feast; the older son rejects the father's pleading but still gets everything that's left of the inheritance.

The father's sole concern is the unity of the family. His favorite Bible verse: "Look at how good and pleasing it is / when families live together as one!" (Psalm 133:1).

Both sons are given an equal share of the father's legacy (Luke 15:12). The father has (shockingly) no interest in morality, propriety, justice, or fairness. All the father wants is a reunified family. The father doesn't desire penitence, respect, or gratitude from his children. His desire is for all of the family to be together at the party.

Where is father at the end of the story? Outside in the dark, with the older brother, pleading with him to let down his proud righteousness and come in to the party.

"What do you expect to receive from a sermon?" I asked my congregation. The predominant answer: "I want a sermon that shows me where I may have gone wrong and then tells me how to go right, motivating me to be a better person."

In other words, we come to church to hear about ourselves, hoping to receive a gentle nudge to be the good person we know ourselves capable of becoming. A sermon is a motivational speech to spur people forward in their moral progress, to shove themselves closer to God, or to tell them what they need to do to earn a more meaningful, happy life.

Church is where we come to receive our assignment for the week: This week, church, work on your sexism, racism, ageism. Come back next week and your preacher promises to lay another to-do list on you. Because after all, it's up to you to do right or right won't be done. You've got the world's future in your hands. Please stand for the Benediction. Now get out there and get busy!

If that's your expectation for sermons or your idea of church, then the riddles of Jesus will sound strange. You may have noted that Jesus's parables are primarily stories about God and only secondarily or derivatively are they stories about us. The parables could not care less about answering questions like, How can I use this to make my life worth living? What am I supposed to do to take hold of my life and become the person I'd like to be? Will this help me to ease my aches and pains?

The parables almost always and everywhere speak about God. Who is God? What is God up to? Since I can't make my life, much less the world, turn out right, what has God done and what's God doing right now to get the world that God wants?

Most of Jesus's parables are surprising because they are talking about a God who is unforeseen and unexpected. Once Jesus had told these stories, the name "God" was forever rendered problematic.

We tend to make "God" fuzzy, vague, and ethereal, an unknowable spiritual blur. That way we can define "God" as we please. But after Jesus rendered God as an actively, recklessly seeking shepherd, searching woman, prodigal father, never again were we free to make "God" mean anything we found personally comfortable. After Jesus's parables, "God" could never denote our nation's patron, blesser of our culture's values, defender of our borders, excuser for my sins, or comforter of my pains, prejudices, and politics.

Who is God and what's God up to? "God" is the proper name for the One who thought up and then hurled at us the parable of the Prodigal Son, no matter the damage done to our idolatries.

"Hey, are you talking about *me?*" we ask indignantly.

Jesus responds, "I'm talking about my heavenly Father, who is also your best friend and only hope."

Please note that only after a parable has talked about God (otherwise known as "reality") does a parable imply or suggest implications for how we ought to live now that Jesus has let us in on the truth about God. Once Jesus depicts God as the seeking shepherd, the searching woman, the celebrating father, it's as if storyteller Jesus says, *Now that you know who God is and what God's up to, don't you want to hitch on to what God is doing? Come, assume the role that God has assigned you in God's relentlessly determined, seeking, searching, celebrating salvation of God's world. Even you can be part of the kingdom of heaven!*

"Wow. You've made quite a turnaround," I said to a young pastor. Earlier, he had told me that he had been struggling with depression because of the sad state of his dwindling congregation. But when I checked on him, a couple of months later, he was visibly energetic, filled with enthusiasm for his work."

What happened?

"I was sitting in my study at the church, just staring out the window," he explained. "Then (maybe it was the prodding of the Holy Spirit) I just stood up, walked out of the church, and took a right down the sidewalk. Something prodded me to start knocking on the doors of our neighbors and saying, 'Hello. I'm the pastor of the church down the street. I wanted to meet you and see how you are doing.' That's all.

"With one exception, everyone opened their door to me and invited me in. I offered to have prayer with each person, asking them for what they would like me to pray for. The second home I visited, the person said, 'I thought that church had closed. Glad to hear it's still open and happy to meet you.'

"I've now covered four blocks in each direction from the church and have met some of the most fascinating folks. Invited some of our lay leaders to visit with me. Our Sunday attendance has nearly doubled."

Then he reflected, "Turns out, Jesus was already active in our neighborhood. Our insularity, lethargy, stay-at-home attitude was the problem. Not Jesus."

About the same time, I received a letter complaining about one of my pastors in the eastern part of our annual conference. "That preacher you sent us is an embarrassment. He is known to be in a bar here in town one or two nights a week! It's not just a bar, it's one of those bars. We don't want a pastor who is hanging out in places like that. You have got to send us a different preacher."

I called the pastor and told him about the letter. "They told the truth," he responded. "I'm in that bar once, sometimes twice a week. Just set up shop at one of the tables and talk to whoever will talk to me. Eight till midnight. Had some of the best theological conversations with folks around the table. Some of them have been badly wounded by the church. Others of them just need some correct information about Jesus.

"I'm a true evangelical. My job isn't just to care for the faithful few, I've got to be out amongst those Jesus wants to be part of our church. I've baptized two folks I met in that bar. More are sure to come."

Then, he said with all seriousness, "Bishop, if you want me to stay away from that place, you are going to figure out how to keep Jesus out of that bar."

The seeking shepherd, the searching woman, the welcoming father, the determined host of the banquet will be out-and-about in the world, joyfully, relentlessly seeking until the lost have been found, every seat at the table is occupied, and the party is in full swing. The evangelistic, missional question is, *Will we?*

So there you have it. In one chapter of Luke's Gospel three parables in a row of a seeking shepherd, a searching woman, and a waiting father where there's searching, forgiveness, restoration, and joy, great, raucous joy. All the way back in Luke 5:32, Jesus was up front about his mission to seek and to save the lost. He'll have to repeat it in 19:10 where we grumble again when Jesus goes to be "a guest at the house of a man who is a sinner."

Over the years, some commentators have questioned the sincerity of the returning son's repentance. Is the prodigal really, truly sorry for what he has done in wasting half of the father's fortune? Is his speech genuine or just due to his desperate need for a meal?

Their questions are beside the point of this parable. Though we may feel the need to judge a returning, repenting sinner's sincerity, the father shows no interest in ascertaining the authenticity of his son's repentance. Jesus said he told the stories of the lost sheep and the lost coin to show that there's more joy in heaven over one sinner's repentance than over all the so-called righteous who think they're not lost and don't need repentance. These stories are not warnings to us to straighten up, fly right, and repent. They are stories about God, about the joy in heaven when one of the lost is found.

The lost sheep and the lost coin didn't "repent." They just got found. Repentance is not the chief note of these parables. It's the parties. All you must do to get close to God is to be willing to be welcomed, hugged, and then come to the party. The younger brother never got to deliver his penitent speech; he just got a party and a really nice pair of shoes. The older brother didn't earn the Young Business Leader of the Year citation; he just got the father, pleading with him to come to the feast.

And yet, like refusing an invitation to a feast in the previous story of the Great Banquet, just being invited isn't the end of the story. The father's pleading is an altar call, an invitation to come, join in God's kingdom. Being found is the beginning of life, not the end of the story. To be a lost sheep who refuses to be found and restored to the sheepfold, or an older brother who stubbornly, proudly insists on standing outside, alone, is to be just like all those sad, lonely ones who refused the master's invitation to the Great Banquet.

Have a good time home alone on the sofa, counting your virtues while you eat microwaved bean burritos and watch reruns of *The Apprentice*.

The older brother's righteously indignant, works-righteousness speech, "All this time have I served you . . ." is as beside the point as his prodigal brother's declaration of repentance. The surprising, outrageous character in this parable is the father and his extravagant welcome to the party.

I know you are accustomed to calling this the prodigal (wasteful, extravagant, loose living) son but will you agree that the most interesting character in the story is the prodigally gracious, welcoming father? By the end of story, both sons, as we, must deal with the father. The father has the last word. To the younger, the father gives embrace and gracious welcome, to the older, reassurance and gracious welcome. You are always with me. All that I have is yours.

Jesus ends the story of the father and two sons without tying everything up with a satisfying conclusion. Did the younger son learn from his errors and straighten up, buy a mini-van and vote Republican the rest of his life? Did the older brother finally loosen up and join the party and find someone willing to listen to him drone on about sound agricultural management? Jesus doesn't say.

Maybe each of us, in our own lives and families, in our own churches and neighborhoods, is finishing the story. We don't know if the wandering, wayward ones will realize that God isn't into keeping score or setting high the moral bar for them to chin up to. Will the I've-been-a-member-of-this-church-all-my-life party poopers loosen up and celebrate the returning Johnny-come-latelies to the Kingdom as our treasured siblings in Christ? Who knows?

Because of the stories of the sheep that's found and coin that's recovered, we now know for sure that God isn't just love; God is seeking, searching, active love that beats the bushes until we are found and returned. What we know for certain is that heaven is poised to break forth into raucous rejoicing whenever any of the lost is found. God is determined to have a unified human family and won't stop the inviting and the pleading until all are gathered in.

What do we have to do to be part of that great godly celebration? Simply let ourselves be loved, invited to a party we didn't deserve, given an inheritance we didn't earn.

And then what do we do? At the end of Luke's Gospel the risen Christ, teller of these tales, commissions his followers, all of them, to be evangelists. It's our job to tell "all nations" the good news of a feast that begins with "a change of heart and life for the forgiveness of sins" (Luke 24:47). He calls us "witnesses," making each of us into servants who deliver the Master's invitation to the feast, sowers who sling the seed, shepherds who seek a lost sheep, women who search for a lost coin, those who open the door and say, "This feast is for you."

Our duty as citizens of God's kingdom? Search. Find. Forgive. Celebrate. Repeat.

My denomination is centuries old. Our ranks have thinned precipitously in the years since I was ordained. (I'm not making a connection between those two events. I'm just saying. . . .) How come the tacky megachurch outside of town—that looks like a movie theater and sounds on Sunday morning like a dance hall on Saturday night, led by a preacher who wears jeans and a T-shirt and got his degree online—is growing and we're not?

I grumble, "Lo these two hundred years we have been working for the Kingdom. We have been obedient to you, mostly. And you never gave us a full parking lot. But when these latecomers, these superficially biblical, theological goofs put up a website and . . . You . . ."

Seeking, searching Jesus had to go all the way out to Gehenna, the city garbage dump to find a lost soul, taking his place beside the thief on the cross. Even while writhing in agony on that dark Friday afternoon, when the thief begged, "Remember me when you come into your kingdom," Jesus invited the convicted felon that day into paradise (Luke 23:42-43).

Resurrected and ascended, on his way to take his seat at the right hand of God, surely the Son was asked by the Father, "What have you got to show for your service, the sermons you preached, the multitudes you healed, your suffering and dying?"

The Son proudly put forth his trophy: one poorly informed, somewhat repentant, nameless thief. Christ's grand achievement, validation of his ministry, justification for his cross.

Joyful that the Son had so well slung the seed, lifted the wounded and dying out of death's ditch, delivered the Father's invitation to the feast, and gathered twelve sinners at the table for one last meal, heaven went wild. One who was lost has been found, one who was dead has been made alive.

Chapter 4
CRUMBS FROM THE TABLE

At a succession of meals, feasts, and parties, Jesus has earned his reputation for eating, drinking, and carousing with sinners. Want to be a citizen of the kingdom of God? Be a certified, undeniable sinner. Allow yourself to be invited to God's Great Banquet.

"For us and for our salvation, he came down from heaven," says the Nicene Creed. Way down. To be "saved" is to join a table full of sinners, some come early, some late, some whose sin is in their sinful lifestyle, and others whose sin is "God, I give you thanks that I have never lived a sinful lifestyle," to quote a Pharisee from another parable (Luke 18:9-14). Salvation: Sinners eating and drinking with Jesus at his Last Supper.

Only God can set things right between you and God. All you need to do to be rescued is to be dying in a ditch. Would you like an invitation to God's table? Be famished. Want to be saved? Get lost. Admit that you're honest-to-God hungry (and aren't we all?). Be somebody in bad need of an invitation to a feast.

Come, all you siblings, be you younger or older, smug religious experts, or wayward, wandering sheep, Pharisees, whores, Methodist preachers, and old guys who write Lenten study books, have I got some good news for you: *bon appétit!* The check has been paid by the host.

Which makes it all the more curious that Luke begins his account of the many mealtimes with Jesus with a somber account of Jesus refusing to eat. Jesus prepared for his ministry by retreating into the wilderness for a forty-day fast: "He ate nothing during those days and afterward Jesus was starving" (Luke 4:2).

There, in the wilderness, the devil makes a rare appearance, taking advantage of Jesus's hunger, tempting him with, "Since you are God's Son, command this stone to become a loaf of bread" (Luke 4:3). Your forty days of hunger are suffered by many every day. Mr. Compassion, Mr. Messianic Miracle Worker, turn stones to bread.

It's the church's custom to tell the story of the Temptation of Christ on the First Sunday of Lent as we begin our forty-day walk with Jesus to Maundy Thursday. Before you head out for the Last Supper, got time for a three-point, First Sunday of Lent sermon?

1. In a Gospel where Jesus goes from one joyous feast to another, it's curious that Luke begins Jesus's journey with the temptations occasioned by hunger.

2. Jesus may be the Son of God, as the voice said at his baptism, but he is still fully, truly human (Luke 3:21-32). He has bodily hunger just like the rest of

us. He knows what it's like to have a "hungry heart" (theologian, Bruce Springsteen).

3. Turning stones into bread? Who could object to Wonder bread? Think of the good that could be done by making bread from stones. And yet, Jesus refuses, quoting scripture: *"People won't live only by bread"* (Luke 4:4). While Jesus will, in his subsequent ministry, repeatedly, miraculously, have compassion for and feed the hungry (Luke 9:12-17), as much as he cares about human, bodily need for bread, Jesus appears to have some greater goal even than compassionate catering.

End of sermon.

Isn't it ironic that bread—utterly necessary staff of life, one of the great pleasures of being human (at least the bread baked by Patsy Parker Willimon), and a necessary ingredient at any banquet worthy of the name—is not the most important part of life? Can hunger for bread, the use and abuse of bread, be an enticement to sin?

Gluttony, sin of the stomach, is one of the Seven Deadlies. And yet as I have found when I'm dieting, it's hard to cut back on food intake. We must eat to live. The utterly necessary for survival, perfectly natural hunger so easily becomes the craving that consumes, causing us to stumble. Some perish from too little bread, others of us are undone by too much. Interesting, huh? Food is a gift of God. We may not live by bread alone, but we don't live long without it either. Yet for some of us, overindulgence becomes our undoing. Sex, money, bread, wine, all good gifts of God yet when abused, used in self-gratifying ways that violate God's intentions, are occasions for sin. For most of us, sin isn't doing something bad; it's abusing an otherwise good gift of God.

Satan proposed "Turn stones to bread" as material demonstration of Jesus's divinity. What the masses crave, Satan implies, is not discipleship, Bible verses, sacrifice, risk, and pain; they want bread and circuses, miracles and power. Turn stones to bread!

Jesus's response? No.

I remind you that hunger and its fulfillment occasioned the fall of our primal parents back in the garden of Eden. They saw that the forbidden tree had "delicious food" so they "took some of its fruit and ate it" (Genesis 3:6).

Jesus's parables connect feasting with God's kingdom; in the temptation, Luke connects food with Satan's wiles. In just a little while the one who began his earthly ministry by refusing to turn stones to bread will end his ministry by turning bread into his body.

Having gotten into hot water for eating and drinking with sinners, Jesus now tells a dirty little parable where bread—how we get it, what we do with it, how having more than we need of it, as well as failing to notice our fellow human beings who lack it—implicates in our damnation.

Some have described a parable as an "earthly story with heavenly meaning." Jesus will now tell us a heavenly story with a helluva earthly meaning:

> *There was a certain rich man who clothed himself in purple and*
> *fine linen, and who feasted luxuriously every day. At his gate*

lay a certain poor man named Lazarus who was covered with
sores. Lazarus longed to eat the crumbs that fell from the rich
man's table. Instead, dogs would come and lick his sores.

(Luke 16:19-21)

Yuck. Jesus goes into excruciating (in the literal sense of that word) detail: oozing sores, starvation, dogs (not house pets, wild street dogs, scourge of the ancient world) licking a poor man's wounds. Jesus's contrast between the worlds of these two people couldn't be more stark.

The poor man for whom each day was a living hell lay just outside the front door of a nameless "rich man" for whom every day was a heavenly great banquet. "Feasted luxuriously" (in the Greek, "making merry, having a ball") is the same word used in two earlier parables (Luke 12:19; 15:23-24, 29). What in the stories of the Great Banquet and the Prodigal Son were extravagant, celebratory special events is an everyday meal for the "certain rich man."

"Lazarus longed to eat the crumbs that fell from the rich man's table. Instead, dogs would come and lick his sores." Has the gap between the rich and poor ever been more harshly drawn?

Eighty-five of the richest people in the world own as much as the poorest 3.5 billion people. The six heirs to Wal-Mart have more money than the poorest 48.8 million American families put together. And you thought that the Bible is irrelevant to our contemporary world!

Sorry if you are uncomfortable with criticism of the wealthiest 1 percent, or if you smell some sort of socialist class-conflict being fomented here, or if you're suspicious that you're going to hear a lecture on the perils of rule by oligarchs. Jesus is determined to tell us a story that pits rich against poor whether we, or they, like it or not.

The rich man is nameless. If you've met one of these fat-cats, you've met them all. By hook, crook, or inheritance, they've accumulated a lot of stuff.

The pitifully poor man, Lazarus, is the only person in all the parables who gets a name. That tells you something about how Jesus meant to highlight him. Though ignored by the "certain rich man," Lazarus is noticed and named by Jesus. *Lazarus* means "One whom God helps," a clue to the significance of this story. So, once again, we're not hearing a riddle about us, the rich and the poor, rather we're confronted by a story of a God who's got this thing for helping the poor and putting one over on the rich.

Poor Lazarus lies in misery at the gate (The Greek word suggests that Lazarus doesn't just lie there; he's been "dumped" there.) (Luke 16:20). The gate separating the two is closed from the inside. The rich man had the opportunity to help. Yet his lifestyle has made Lazarus invisible. He doesn't oppress or abuse Lazarus. He simply never sees him.

You may recall that back at the Pharisee's table (Luke 7:44), vision, noticing was the problem there too: "Do you see this woman?" Jesus asked. The Samaritan, on the other hand, noticed and, in seeing, stopped to help the man in the ditch. The father wanted the older brother to see that "your brother that was lost has been found." The Lord of the banquet saw those who lived in the alleyways as fit recipients for his invitation to the feast. Would that the rich man could open his eyes to the one who lies outside his gated community. This parable doesn't rise to the level of an exhortation to risk, to begin a ministry to the food deprived, or to go forth and transform food deserts; all it asks is for us to open our eyes and see beyond our gates. Notice.

If you want to avoid the claim of those on the sidewalk begging you for a handout, take care not to look at their eyes.

Then a joke is played on the rich and the poor:

> *The poor man died and was carried by angels to Abraham's side. The rich man also died and was buried. While being tormented in the place of the dead, he looked up and saw Abraham at a distance with Lazarus at his side. He shouted, "Father Abraham, have mercy on me. Send Lazarus to dip the tip of his finger in water and cool my tongue, because I'm suffering in this flame." But Abraham said, "Child, remember that during your lifetime you received good things, whereas Lazarus received terrible things. Now Lazarus is being comforted and you are in great pain. Moreover, a great crevasse has been fixed between us and you. Those who wish to cross over from here to you cannot. Neither can anyone cross from there to us."*
>
> *(Luke 16:22-26)*

Job 21:26 says the rich and the poor have one thing in common: "Together they lie down in the dust; worms cover them both." Of all the parables Jesus tells, this is the only one that depicts any details of the afterlife. The main characteristic of eternity: The life to come will be a dramatic turning of the tables for the rich and the poor (Luke 16:19-26). No speculation or specification for why the two men end up in different places. It can't simply be that the man was rich because, after all, Abraham himself was very rich. However, unlike the nameless rich man,

Abraham was a model of hospitality when he entertained three strangers, one of whom happened to be the Lord (Genesis 18:1-15). But that's another story.

While the parable avoids speculation on exactly why the rich man is made to suffer torment in Hades or why Lazarus lies safe, cherished in Abraham's bosom, the rich man's dialogue with Father Abraham offers some justification: "Child, remember that during your lifetime you received good things, whereas Lazarus received terrible things. Now Lazarus is being comforted and you are in great pain. Moreover, a great crevasse has been fixed between us and you. Those who wish to cross over from here to you cannot. Neither can anyone cross from there to us" (Luke 16:25-26).

Hey, insensitive, gated, rich man who never made eye contact "with the less fortunate", your riches gave you heaven on earth, life as good as it gets. What could God add to your lavish feasts? Now, it's Lazarus's turn.

In death, Lazarus is carried to a place of honor beside Abraham, father of Israel. The rich man (unsurprisingly to us, since we've been listening to Luke's parables and know that the rich are in big trouble) is surprised to wake up in Hades, place of heat, torment, and punishment (Luke 10:15). [4]

The rich man, who had no contact with the poor across the economic crevasse in life, for the first time, at last sees Lazarus across a great gap in the life hereafter (Luke 16:24-26). The rich man in Hades doesn't address Lazarus. He is still too isolated to notice. He pleads with Abraham to send Lazarus to succor his torment. That's what rich people do; send those with fewer means to run our errands. Abraham refuses.

In life, Lazarus suffered bad things; now the tables are turned. Lazarus is comforted; the rich man is in agony. It would have been nice if the rich man had reached across the wealth gap in this world to give Lazarus a hand. Sorry. Too late. Now we're in the next world and a "great chasm" now exists between the two, a gap over which no one can pass, even to dip his finger in water to help the rich man's misery.

In life, the rich man failed to open his eyes, to connect, to reach out across the chasm between the rich and the poor. In this world's kingdoms, we look upon riches as a way to gain security, opportunities, and independence, to buy a seat at the table. But in God's kingdom, riches keep us out of the feast, trapped, in the dark, blinding us to the needs of others, missing the opportunity to live the lives for which God has created us. In short, sin.

By the time the rich man notices Lazarus, it's too late.

There's more:

> *The rich man said, "Then I beg you, Father, send Lazarus to my father's house. I have five brothers. He needs to warn them so that they don't come to this place of agony." Abraham replied, "They have Moses and the Prophets. They must listen to them." The rich man said, "No, Father Abraham! But if someone from the dead goes to them, they will change their hearts and lives." Abraham said, "If they don't listen to Moses and the Prophets, then neither will they be persuaded if someone rises from the dead."*
>
> *(Luke 16:27-31)*

The rich man entreats Abraham for himself, then he pleads for the rest of his close family, the limit of his compassion. Send

Lazarus to warn my five brothers about their coming fate in Hades (Luke 16:27-31). Abraham is dismissive: Aw, they've always had Moses and the prophets who repeatedly hammered the rich and pled for the poor. (After idolatry, riches are the main target of the prophets' ire.) This is news to your buddies back at the club? What do you want? Somebody to die, rise from the dead, go to hell, preach again to your brothers what anybody who's ever heard anything God's been saying through the prophets ought to already know? Forget it.

At this point, it shouldn't surprise us that Jesus has no difficulty in contrasting the sorry fate of the rich with the eventual blessing of the poor or in preaching that God's coming kingdom brings about a marked reversal of the status of the haves and the have-nots. In Luke's Sermon on the Plain, Jesus clearly announced to the poor that the kingdom of God belongs to them, combining it with a warning to the rich that their future will be grim because they have already received their consolation (Luke 6:20-25). Consolation for the poor; woe to the rich is Jesus from start to finish.

Excursus: The Greek word that is translated as *consolation* in Jesus's sermon in Luke 6:24 (KJV) shares the same root as the word that describes Lazarus's comfort in Luke 16:25. God is not only love but also justice. God is neither neutral nor passive when it comes to wealth and poverty. Which is to say that whereas nine of this parable's twelve verses take place in either heaven or hell, most of their relevance is for right here on earth. Now that you know your eternal destination, don't all you rich want to jump on board God's kingdom express right now? Consumption, as good as it often is, has no place in God's kingdom, which is big on mercy, reparations, and consolation. The gate, your fancy security system by which you lock out the poor, has become your prison. Your fancy lifestyle is not only bad for your cholesterol count, it's hell on your soul too. If you are squeamish about money talk or defensive about the size of your investment portfolio, don't ask Jesus to say a word at the funeral.

Riches are a blessing and also an assignment, preached Jesus. "Much will be demanded from everyone who has been given much, and from the one who has been entrusted with much, even more will be asked" (Luke 12:48). It would have been good if the rich man would have opened his eyes to Lazarus, seeing him as a fellow "child of Abraham." Even better if he had opened his wallet, seeing the need of brother as a responsibility.

Think of the Samaritan who

was on a journey, [and] came to where the man was. But when he saw him, he was moved with compassion. The Samaritan went to him and bandaged his wounds, tending them with oil and wine. Then he placed the wounded man on his own donkey, took him to an inn, and took care of him. The next day, he took two full days' worth of wages and gave them to the innkeeper. He said, "Take care of him, and when I return, I will pay you back for any additional costs".

(Luke 10:33-35)

The Samaritan was, one presumes, rich. Jesus makes a Samaritan man of means the hero of his story, not because of his possessions but rather because he "saw" the victim in the ditch and responded to the stranger's need effusively, "with compassion," using his means to help another, making no demand upon the man he aided.

See? Jesus doesn't despise people with money; he just thinks he has the right to tell us how to spend it.

Back in Nazareth at his first sermon, Jesus declares that the Spirit of the Lord is upon him "to preach good news to the poor" (Luke 4:18). And we've already heard Jesus end the story of the Great Banquet by advising his followers not to invite their neighbors who can repay them, but to invite the poor, the crippled, the lame, and the blind (Luke 14:13).

Later, Jesus will tell a parable of the Great Judgment in which treatment of the hungry and thirsty, strangers, the naked, the sick, and those in prison is linked to an eternal fate (Matthew 25:31-46).

Neither we nor the rich man and his five brothers are eager to hear either Abraham or Jesus tell another story involving wealth and poverty. But the story that is for many of us bad news is for somebody like Lazarus the gospel.

Although as a preacher I've used (abused?) this parable to encourage better stewardship (i.e., give more to the church budget), this story doesn't have much to do with tithing. Nor is there any direct encouragement of generosity to the poor. The rich man shows no animosity toward Lazarus, nor does he actively abuse him. The rich man just sits there, engorging himself with the bounty of God's gifts, praise the Lord, every day my own personal, individual great banquet, heaven on earth, as good as it gets. Living his best life now. God is so good, pass the caviar. Thank you, Jesus.

The rich man bears no ill will toward Lazarus; he just doesn't see him. Indifferent "to the brother dumped" outside the gate. Unable or unwilling to open his eyes.

Sin as a failure to see.

Preach this parable and I guarantee somebody in the congregation will respond, if they have the guts to say it, "I don't come to church to be made to look at, or to hear talk about, unpleasant things like this." Unless you have a congregation where there's a chance that a Lazarus might be present.

No virtues are ascribed to Lazarus. The poor man displays no animosity toward the inequality and injustice of the world; he just isn't seen. He says not a word and does nothing to gain entrance into the bosom of Father Abraham; his only attribute is desperately to need merciful healing and a good meal which, according to Jesus, he will receive at last.

Once again, we're hearing a parable that's primarily about who God is and what God has created God's world to be, and where the world is, by God, headed. Only by implication are we urged to be or do. In the parable, Jesus does not scold or prescribe; he describes. This is the God of whom the psalmist asks,

> *Who could possibly compare to the LORD our God?*
> *God rules from on high;*
> *he has to come down to even see heaven and earth!*
> *God lifts up the poor from the dirt*
> *and raises up the needy from the garbage pile.*
> *(Psalm 113:5-7)*

God did not create our economy of rich and poor. If you happen to be like Lazarus, for whom this world has been life on a garbage pile, sing Psalm 113:5-7 and take heart. You may not know where to find your next meal, or how to gain access to health care, or how to keep a roof over your head but at least you know who is God. God comes down, lifts up the poor, and raises up the needy from where we—the anonymous, uncaring, unmerciful, gated rich—fail to see that we have any responsibility to join with God in raising "up the poor from the dirt" and the "garbage pile" where they have been dumped.

The poor are lifted up by God, not because they are good, but because they are low and because God lifts the lowly. The poor respond to God (accept the invitation to the Banquet, come inside to God's party, allow themselves to be lifted out of the ditch) because they've got no hope but God.

Mary said it best. Who is God? God is the one who,

> *has pulled the powerful down from their thrones*
> *and lifted up the lowly.*
> *He has filled the hungry with good things*
> *and sent the rich away empty-handed.*
>
> (Luke 1:52-53)

Albert Schweitzer, when asked why he gave up his career as a famous organist and status as a German professor to go to Africa as a medical missionary, answered, "Out there in the colonies sits wretched Lazarus."

As we said at the beginning of this journey with Jesus, if you are going to walk with him, you'll have to listen to his stories. You may recall another story that Jesus told where the joke was on the rich man who thought he had it made. With full barns and a fat bank account, he told himself to take it easy and to enjoy his entrepreneurial success. We would eulogize him as a successful, prudent businessman. God's angel of death addressed him as "Fool" (Luke 12:13-21).

But that's another story.

Wouldn't you know it? The Revised Common Lectionary pairs 1 Timothy 6:9-10 with the story of Lazarus and the rich man. Paul, say something to the more materially blessed in the congregation:

> People who try to get rich fall into temptation. They are trapped by many stupid and harmful passions that plunge people into ruin and destruction. The love of money is the root of all kinds of evil. Some have wandered away from the faith and have impaled themselves with a lot of pain because they made money their goal.
>
> (1 Timothy 6:9-10)

Ouch.

That's why if your take-home pay is as much as mine, you may want to call in sick on the Third Sunday of September, Year C.

I know a church that voted to leave the denomination that birthed their congregation because they felt that leaders of the denomination had violated one of the three or four possible biblical verses excluding same-sex practices. "We stand on the Bible," they boasted. "Enough of liberal, mainline, mealymouth softness on sin. We're going to name sin when we see it."

I listened to over a hundred video sermons preached in that congregation. Not one word from their pulpit on the *two thousand* verses in Scripture on the evil of riches. They left, taking their sixty-million dollar church property with them, claiming that their love of Jesus made them do it.

In the light of Luke 16, they've got some explaining to do.

Luke puts down the Pharisees as "lovers of money" (Luke 16:14). The rich young man asks Jesus how he can inherit eternal life only to have Jesus tell him to sell all he has and distribute the money to the poor. He climbed back into his leather-seated Porsche and left, leading Jesus to remark that it's real hard to save rich people. How hard is it, Jesus? As hard as shoving a fully loaded camel through the eye of a needle (Luke 18:18-30).

That's hard.

A rich man whom the world might call prudent, Jesus names as a fool (Luke 12:8-21). Possessions are to be sold and the wealth is to be distributed to the poor (Luke 12:33; 18:22). After Jesus proclaims that "salvation has come" to the house of rich Zacchaeus, the chief tax collector gives half of his possessions to the poor and repays anyone he has defrauded four times as much (Luke 19:1-10). Luke's second volume, The Acts of the Apostles, claims that the first Christians would "sell pieces of property and possessions and distribute the proceeds to everyone who needed them. . . . They shared food with gladness and simplicity" (Acts 2:45-46).

G. K. Chesterton is reputed to have said that we could have a good debate on whether or not Jesus believed in fairies. He was a first-century man. Lots of people back then believed in fairies. Did Jesus?

One thing that's not up for debate is if Jesus believed that rich people were in big trouble. He told too many stories to leave any doubt.

As Christians, we can have disagreements about what to do to fix the wealth gap. Who to tax and how much. However, there can be no disagreement that Jesus takes sides, that he has clearly set up the argument in such a way as to indicate that God is not mocked, that God will work justice for the poor whether we do or not, that in God's future there will be a price to be paid by those who have enjoyed life's luxuries and blessedness and denied to their neighbors basic human needs like food, housing, and health care (three of the necessities that were denied the poor man).

Tell me if you can figure out any other way to interpret this little story from Jesus.

But let's be clear (and it seems to me this parable is very clear), the Christian position is always open-eyed concern for those who have less and a sense of judgment and responsibility for those of us who have more. I'm not being a class warfare, political correctness, socialist leaning, tax-and-spend liberal, I'm just telling you what we can't avoid thinking if we listen to Jesus.

Excursus: On the few times that I've had the guts to preach this parable, or the many passages like it, a frequent response is, "Well, all that might be in the Bible, but programs for the poor just won't work. The welfare system is broken. Redistribution of wealth isn't realistic. It sounds downright Socialist. The real world isn't like that, etc., etc."

Tell it to Jesus. He thinks he's talking about the "real world," that is, the world as God intends it to be, the realm that God is moving us toward, sooner or later, aka, the kingdom of heaven.

If you have detected a tad of defensiveness in my presentation of the parable of the rich man in Hades, you are right. I've never had to worry where my children's next meal came from. I don't live in a gated community, but I live a long way from the Lazaruses of Durham. I've always thought of my situation as attributable to my hard work, having been raised in an industrious family, or just good luck. Never thought about my lot as "sin," until Jesus brought it up.

Because of my economic circumstances, this story sounds like bad news. I've preached sermons on this text, but it took a lot of fancy interpretive footwork for me to do so: None of us are all that rich. I wear tweed to dinner parties, not purple. I volunteer once a month with Habitat for Humanity. I voted Democratic in the last election. Every Christmas, I write a check to Durham Urban Ministry.

See? This news is not so bad after all, if you are paying enough to have a preacher like me to get you off the hook.

I'm defensive because I assume that there's nobody reading this book who would hear Jesus's story as anything but judgment, condemnation, and bad news.

But if you are one of those who is often absent from or invisible to our affluent congregations, that is, somebody who can relate to how it feels to be Lazarus, then this story's for you. If you have known sickness in a world that worships health, poverty in a world where people's worth is judged by how much money they can accumulate, emptiness and hunger in a culture where many perish from too much to eat rather than too little, has Jesus got some good news for you.

And even for those of us who have known relative riches, there is some good news. Our material blessings are indeed blessings. And yet, the story suggests that they become curses when they are abused as ways to widen the gap between those of us who have more and those who have less, or as blinders to our siblings in Christ. God's intentions (as we saw in the story of the Prodigal Son) are for a unified family. We are not created to be divided, separated from one another in gated communities and economically segregated neighborhoods. We are created for communion, made to take responsibility for people who are not in our families, to reach out to sisters and brothers in need across any of the borders the world puts up between us. Both the rich man and Lazarus are family, children of Father Abraham.

That Jesus Christ, bearer of the good news of God's coming kingdom, tells stories that sound like bad news to some of us may be a commentary, not on the bad news of Jesus, but rather on the way we huddle together in sanctified clubs full of folks in our tax bracket, calling that "church."

It's too late for the rich man. And yet, if we are listening to this story, it's not too late for us. Here we are, listening to Jesus hurl a tough story at us that calls into question our definitions of success and the good life, a story that gives us a glimpse into the future so that maybe we might live our lives differently in the present, a snapshot of future heaven and hell that enables us to see the present world differently.

The rich man didn't see Lazarus and felt no responsibility toward him, nor did the one who feasted every day and who dressed in purple listen to the clear words of Moses and the prophets.

But as for you, Jesus made you look. He has told you a story you didn't want to hear, forced you to stare at a great chasm between the rich and the poor that you might have previously missed. Social distancing overcome by Jesus.

Surprise. Father Abraham was wrong. Somebody has come back from the dead to tell us the truth about the future and to show us our true situation. Jesus comes back from the grave and returns to us on Sunday to us to show us the peril of our riches and also to give us something good to do with our wealth.

Good news. You know the truth. It's too late for the rich man in the parable, but it's not too late for you. There's still time to live the truth rather than the lie that masquerades as The American Dream, the sin that we prefer to name as You Earned It, You Deserve It, You Can Keep It. Open your eyes, as we pass the offering plate on Sunday and you are given the opportunity to shell out for the needs of others who are not in your family, as you take responsibility for someone else's pain even though you don't know their name. Good news: You not only know the truth; you're doing it.

What you put in the plate at church is not the whole journey outside of your gated community, but it's a good first step.

Abraham underestimated the power of Jesus's resurrection. Here you are listening to me listen to crucified and resurrected Jesus tell you a story. Surprise. Somebody has come back from the dead and you are listening even when what he's got to say is hard to hear.

By God's grace, there's still time for Jesus, Abraham, Lazarus, and the Rich Man to come back from the dead just in time to warn us. And there's still time for us to heed their warning.

Excursus: Heard or preached a sermon on this parable lately? I'd be surprised if you have. It rarely makes our Top Ten lists of Jesus's stories. Guess why.

Our journey toward Maundy Thursday continues. Spoiler alert: At the end, while Jesus was being a host, taking a loaf of bread, breaking it, and offering it to those at the table, one of those at the table was taking a bribe from the authorities to help them arrest Jesus. One of his own followers, a member of the first set of twelve disciples, the inner circle who heard all of Jesus's stories and who shared meals with him, will betray Jesus.

The reason for Judas's dreadful betrayal of his Lord and friend at the Last Supper?

Money.

Admit it. Who among us resentful, envious, middle-class, salt-of-the-earth working folk, doesn't enjoy watching Jesus beat up on the Fortune 500? Stick it to the fat cats, Jesus.

But right after telling the story of Lazarus and the rich man, Jesus goes to Jericho. Bypassing all the humble, down-to-earth folks serving or being served at the church soup kitchen, Jesus invites himself to the home of the richest oligarch in town, Zacchaeus (Luke 19:1-10).

He was a "ruler among tax collectors [and] was rich" (Luke 19:2). Zacchaeus was not only the wee little man who "climbed up a sycamore-fig tree" to see Jesus; he was also a despised capo of the whole gang of thieving tax collectors, fleecing their own people, shaking them down to pay for the Roman occupation forces.

And Zacchaeus was the only person with whom Jesus shared a meal when he went through Jericho.

Pause a moment and let that sink in.

Jesus's self-invite to Zacchaeus's house caused grumbling. Are you surprised? It was rather endearing when Jesus partied with those whores and tax collectors back on the road. He thereby showed what a big heart he had, even for those who weren't saints. Inclusive. Accepting. Affirming. God's DEI program parabolized and personified.

But when Jesus says, "Zacchaeus, come down at once. I must stay in your home today" (Luke 19:5), it's tough for us to take.

Zacchaeus scrambles down out of the tree "happy to welcome Jesus" (Luke 19:6). Let the joyful party begin, this time at the home of the worst sinner in town.

"Everyone who saw this grumbled, saying [a line we've heard before], 'He has gone to be the guest of a sinner'" (Luke 19:7).

A parable: King Jesus returns finally to claim his crown. Where does he first go? To my modest, but neatly kept middle-class neighborhood in Durham, North Carolina? No. He goes right to Washington where he meets with the richest (and therefore most envied and despised), most privileged (having worked the kingdoms of this world to his personal advantage) mob boss in town. A convicted criminal with a gold-plated toilet, I bet.

I guess I've got more in common with the first-century, good, synagogue-going, Jericho grumblers than I first thought, I mutter.

Once lunch is served, before Jesus has a chance to say anything, lay out his program, or tell any of his notorious stories, Zacchaeus taps his Irish lead crystal goblet to propose a toast: "Look, Lord! I give half of my possessions to the poor.

And if I have cheated anyone, I repay them four times as much" (Luke 19:8). Wow. The most dramatic, tangible reparations response that Jesus has received from anybody.

Jesus declares, "Today salvation has come to this household because he too is a son of Abraham. The [let me say it one more time for all you mutterers] Human One came to seek and save the lost. (Luke 9:9). Poor Lazarus rests in Father Abraham's bosom. Rich Zacchaeus rests easy in knowing that he, too, is cherished as a member of Abraham's family.

Zacchaeus's table is one of the few places where Jesus uses the word *salvation*. In this enacted parable, Jesus defines *salvation*: *Whenever Jesus invites himself to your table.* Not someday, somewhere else in eternity, but here, now, "today." Whenever the lost are found. Jesus is not waiting for an invitation; inviting himself to your house. That's "salvation."

We've never been good at coming to God. So, in Jesus Christ, God comes to us, even as he showed up in order to save Zacchaeus.

> *"Look! God's dwelling is here with humankind. He will dwell with them, and they will be his peoples. God himself will be with them as their God. He will wipe away every tear from their eyes. Death will be no more. There will be no mourning, crying, or pain anymore, for the former things have passed away."*
>
> *(Revelation 21:3-4)*

Furthermore (and this is important for the story of Zacchaeus and Jesus), salvation is an undeserved, unearned, unmerited gift *and also* a life-changing, costly assignment. Jesus's love is free, but receiving his love could cost you an arm and a leg. Whenever those who are found and saved respond with specific, material acts of generosity (money) to the poor, making restitution, reparation (plus interest) to any they've cheated, that's "salvation."

Sure you want to be saved by Jesus?

Chapter 5
REFUSING
THE HOST

Right after lunch at the home of the richest, most despised person in town, where Zacchaeus responds to Jesus's salvation with the biggest giveaway Jericho had ever seen, Jesus hits the road toward Jerusalem. On the way, throwing another parable toward them:

As they listened to this, Jesus told them another parable because he was near Jerusalem and they thought God's kingdom would appear right away. He said, "A certain man who was born into royalty went to a distant land to receive his kingdom and then return. He called together ten servants and gave each of them money worth four months' wages. He said, 'Do business with this until I return.' His citizens hated him, so they sent a delegation after him who said, 'We don't want this man to be our king.' After receiving his kingdom, he returned and called the servants to whom he had given the money to find out how much they had earned. *The first servant came forward and said, 'Your money has earned a return of one thousand percent.' The king replied, 'Excellent! You are a good servant. Because you have been faithful in a small matter, you will have authority over ten cities.'*

The second servant came and said, 'Master, your money has made a return of five hundred percent.' To this one, the king said, 'You will have authority over five cities.'

Another servant came and said, 'Master, here is your money. I wrapped it up in a scarf for safekeeping. I was afraid of you because you are a stern man. You withdraw what you haven't deposited and you harvest what you haven't planted.' The king replied, 'I will judge you by the words of your own mouth, you worthless servant! You knew, did you, that I'm a stern man, withdrawing what I didn't deposit and harvesting what I didn't plant? Why then didn't you put my money in the bank? Then when I arrived, at least I could have gotten it back with interest.'

He said to his attendants, 'Take his money and give it to the one who has ten times as much.' 'But Master,' they said, 'he already has ten times as much!' He replied, 'I say to you that everyone who has will be given more, but from those who have nothing, even what they have will be taken away. As for my enemies who don't want me to be their king, bring them here and slaughter them before me.'"

(Luke 19:11-27)

Geeze. I'm no financier, but it seems like that's harsh punishment merely for bad investing. The king's "servants" have become his "enemies" just because they are overly cautious investors?

Unlike many other parables, we must not too quickly assume that this king is God the Father or Jesus the Son. The words, "bring them here and slaughter them in front of me" wouldn't fit in Jesus's mouth. Thus, some interpreters have said that this ought not to be called the parable of the coins but "the parable of the greedy, cruel king."

Maybe the parable is not a simile ("God's kingdom is similar to..."). Jesus is not saying, here's what God's realm is like but what it's *not* like.

There's little to admire in this king. But not much that's surprising either. It's your same old story of those who grab power and then use it against the powerless. Powerful people climb up to the top, even if they have to travel to "a distant land" to get what they want. They surround themselves with sycophants, lackeys, members of their families, patrons whom they can trust to be servile and tell them what they want to hear. And if their trust is betrayed, there's hell to pay. If any underling dares to tell the truth (I know you to be a "stern man") brace yourself for a deadly temper tantrum from the old man.

The servant who got only one coin (actually a *mina*, a great deal of money) is cautious with what the king gave him; the king is one tough boss for whom return on investment means everything and failure to increase the king's power brings the king's murderous wrath.

Maybe the parable says that worldly kings are *not* divine and our world's ways of doing business are *not* God's way.

The king's language is not only harsh but over the top, hyperbolic. Remember: we're not listening to a direct teaching by Jesus but rather to a parable, an exaggerated story, perhaps overstating things in order to grab our attention, shake us up, and spur us to action.

Luke says that Jesus told this story because some of his followers think that at last the kingdom is coming when finally Jesus casts off this humble rabbi demeanor and steps up and starts acting like a real king (as Satan tempted him to do back in the desert). At last Jesus will seize power, give his enemies what they deserve, and take us back to the glory days of the kingdom of David (Acts 1:6).

When we hear "king" applied to Jesus or "God's kingdom" describing what's coming, it's only natural for us to think that we know what is being talked about. Jesus tells this parable a few days before he shall be hailed as "king," but not as the unforgiving, violent, hard-hearted kings of this world. He'll be a "king" on a donkey. Maybe Jesus told this parable to say, in effect, "Come on, haven't we all had enough of these kings and these sorts of kingdoms? Why don't you immigrate and become a citizen of God's kingdom?"

Our sympathies lie with the servant who receives one mina who does what is prudent, responsible, careful, and secure, what any reasonable person would do, that is, what any of us would do.

He says to his king, "I value what you have given me. I greatly fear, er, uh, I mean respect your power and authority. Therefore I didn't want to be reckless. After all, I do not have a broker's license, not even a beginner's class in basic investing. Here's the money you entrusted to me, all safe and sound, once you unwrap that scarf and wipe the dirt off it. Now, tell me what a good boy am I."

The king screams loud enough for everyone in the realm to hear, "You wicked servant! I can't stand the sight of you. You, you miserable little coward! Off with his head!"

The king goes ballistic. Even accounting for the exaggeration of a parable, the king's response is excessive. A story of disproportionate punishment from the imagination of rarely judgmental Jesus meant to grab the attention of those of us who think we can live our lives free of accountability.

The man's defense for burying his mina? "I was afraid of you because you are a stern man. You withdraw what you haven't deposited and you harvest what you haven't planted."

Excuse me. If someone unconditionally dumps this much dough upon you, would you fear him as "a stern man"? Would you call your benefactor a thief who takes money that's not his and reaps where he hasn't sown?

The king has not taken anything from anybody. On the contrary, he has recklessly given a bunch of money to his servants, sowing among them a huge amount of cash without being asked by them to do so. It's only right for the giver to expect some return on his gift. Right?

God's kingdom is like a king who entrusts a huge amount of his money to untrained, untested servants who have no investment experience and no reason to anticipate such generosity. Then the king leaves town.

But when the king returns, it's accountability, judgment time, or celebration of achievements, congratulations, party time, depending on their response to a simple question: *What have you done with what you have been given?*

The one-mina guy doesn't have much to show for himself. He judged the king to be no better than a hardhearted crook with impossible expectations. So he cautiously, fearfully snuck out into his backyard and, after wrapping the money in a scarf, buried the gift he had been given.

Perhaps the king doesn't mind if the recipients of his generosity wastefully put at risk his wealth by investing in bitcoin, or playing the horses at the track, or throwing a huge party for their buddies.

Or feeding the hungry. Or giving it all away to the poor. Or lending a helping hand to somebody down on her luck.

The king responds not with, "I'm proud of you for playing it safe." Rather, the king says, "I will judge you by your own words, you wicked servant! You accuse me of being a tough boss, no better than a common criminal! If you were so frightened of my return, then why didn't you risk, wheel and deal, so that you could have some joy in the discovery that you are an investment genius and I could enjoy some return on my investment in you, you wicked little, timid, unproductive servant? Take that mina away from him and give it to somebody else who knows what to do with a gracious opportunity of a lifetime. Once you wipe the dirt off it."

Be fair to the king before you judge him. All that the king has he has prodigally given to his servants. If they prosper, the king looks good. See what my servants can do once I graciously give them the opportunity to be entrepreneurs!

However, if one takes the king's gift, buries it in the dirt (covering with a ridiculous scarf), the trust that the king has put in his servants will look ridiculous.

Actions, or lack thereof, have consequences. The one-mina servant is the brunt of his master's wrath, not because of the evil that he has done but rather because of the good he didn't do. The good that I ought to do, maybe even sometimes want to do, I don't, laments even Paul (Romans 7:19). "We have done what we ought not to have done and left undone what we should have done," the church once taught us to confess before coming to the Lord's Table.

We are not hard-hearted, active criminals; we are just sparsely talented types who are unimaginative, risk-averse, fearful folk whose prudence and phobias sometimes get the best of us. Sins of omission are a bigger problem than sins of commission when you believe God is a hard-hearted tyrant rather than Jesus Christ.

Maybe you've heard the libelous rumor that God is a stern, judgmental scorekeeper just waiting to catch you screwing up so he can bring the hammer down on you. But what if you heard wrong? What if the king is actually a prodigally generous wheeler-dealer, overly trusting, absurdly generous, and willing to risk everything he's got in order to encourage the prosperity of a bunch of untalented, inexperienced servants?

We sympathize with the one-mina guy because most of us are not multitalented. Neither are most churches I've served. From what I've seen, Jesus has not seen fit to give the church secrets to crafting good legislative policy, or special expertise in making American history turn out right, or the silver bullet that will solve climate change. Jesus has left us with no complex and profound philosophy of life that will wow the intellectually elite, or even sure-fire, knock-down guidelines on how to have a happy life.

All we've been given is one little mina, I mean, gift: *love*. Repeatedly Jesus stressed, Love one another (John 13:34). Love yourself; love your neighbor (Mark 12:31). Love your enemies, even (Matthew 5:43-44). Then he left town. What will we have to show for ourselves when there's an accounting? How will we have invested, wheeling and dealing, the one gift we have been given?

"Maundy Thursday" comes from the Latin word *mandatum*. Commandment. At table with us, just before the cross, Jesus said, "I give you a new commandment: Love each other. Just as I have loved you, so you also must love each other." His last will and testament? Love. His final commandment (not suggestion or recommendation) delivered at the Last Supper? Love (John 13:34).

The church council meeting was tense. The topic under discussion: "What ought we to do with the homeless people who sleep on our church porch every night?" Have you seen refuse in the churchyard? What's our liability? There's been vandalism. Are these people a threat to the safety of our church members? Isn't it time for a security system upgrade?

One of the oldest members said simply, "I don't know just what we ought to do, but I do know that if we make a mistake in what we decide tonight, Jesus commands us to err on the side of love."

We may not be the most impressive church in town, not many among us are dramatic saints. All we've been given is the gift of knowing the truth about who God really is and what God is up to in God's world: love. Let's not play it safe by putting a scarf around it and burying the one precious gift we have been given.

In just a few days after telling of this parable, Jesus will recklessly, prodigally, invest everything he's got at a supper with a bunch of servants like us. All in the name of one little word: *love.*

Rarely does Jesus tell a story because we asked for it. Rather than guarding his truth, he wheels and deals, giving away everything he's got to a bunch of servants, risking it all on the likes of us.

If you are reading this book, following Jesus, attempting to see him more clearly, love him more dearly, and follow him more nearly, it's because some "evangelist"—Sunday school teacher, coach, youth leader, grandmother, person at the office, college roommate—handed over the good news to you, probably before you asked. Aren't you glad they didn't carefully cover it with a scarf, bury it in their backyard, and keep it to themselves?

The gifts of God are also, to those who open-handedly receive the gift of God's salvation of sinners, assignments. The world will know that we know a loving, forgiving God when the world sees some of that love boldly, recklessly invested by us in the world.

The day that the Trump administration ordered ICE to start rounding up immigrants for deportation, a woman in my church called every immigrant she knew, prayed for them over the phone, then told them to call her "if anybody lays a hand on you."

"What would you do if they called and asked for help?" I asked.

"I dunno. Whatever the Lord led me to do, I guess. I can't fix immigration policy and I am no government official. I'm eighty-five years old and can't leave my house except using a walker. I just do what I can do."

Arriving at a little Methodist church in rural Alabama, I was puzzled to see a large sixteen-wheeler parked in the church's small parking lot. "New Oregon UMC" was painted on the side of the truck.

"What's that?" I asked the pastor.

"Our Mission Truck. This church has a tradition of everybody taking off two weeks in the summer and building a house for somebody who needs it. We're on our sixteenth house," he replied. "We're just a little church, just working folks. But we've got enough plumbers, carpenters, bricklayers, and willing hands to partner with Jesus in some good work."

What an answer to, *What have you done with what you've been given?*

Back when I was a college student, there was only one phone on our dormitory hall. If a student wanted to call out of college, it was that phone or nothing. As providence would have it, my room was next to the phone. If I left my dorm room door slightly ajar, I could overhear the conversations:

"Yes ma'am. I know I should have done better."

Silence.

"I know. I thought biology was going to work out better but . . ."

Silence.

"That history professor had it in for me from day one. He was . . ."

Again, silence.

"Okay. I promise. I'm going to do better next semester. I've learned my lesson and ..."

After he ended the conversation, he made it as far as my room, then plopped down on the couch demanding, "Give me a cigarette."

"Parents. They just don't understand. I know how you feel," I said in a show of camaraderie.

"Not sure you do," he replied. "I can see her point."

"Her point?"

"She's working two jobs to pay for me to be here," he explained. "She called me from the lawyer's office she has to clean every night. I guess, the way she sees it, she's putting more into my college education than I am. She's got a right to be pissed."

Before you castigate the king, ask, *Is the king overly, unrealistically, sternly demanding or does the king have ridiculously great faith in, and therefore high expectations for, his servants?*

To us has been given the riches of the gospel, the good news about who God is and what God is up to. We have received into our hands the truth about the inbreaking of the kingdom of God. Jesus has clearly commanded us to be out and about making disciples, wheeling and dealing, investing in others, sharing what we've been given (read Matthew 28, the Great Commission), opening our gates to the Lazaruses in our town. Yet here we sit, hunkered down in a safe sanctuary with folks just like us, people for whom the good news is no longer news. The minas we've been generously given, buried by us, all safe and sound.

Invited to a "Pub Theology" session at a local bar, I was asked to speak on the Trinity. The Trinity? Are you kidding?

My host told me, "Tell these young adults why it's fun to believe that God is triune."

So I did my best to share the riches of Trinitarian faith in a bar full of twenty-somethings.

After I finished, I asked, "Questions?"

Silence. Then one of the young adults blurted, "Why have you guys been keeping all the good stuff to yourselves? This is the first I've heard that God was so much more confusing, interesting, and out of control than I was led to believe when I was a kid."

Take off the silly scarf you've tied around the truth. Scrape off the dirt and wheel and deal. See how much return we can earn on the king's investment in us.

I know, I know. The king in the parable didn't just blow his stack and show disappointment at the financial caution of his one-mina servant. He said, "Bring them [my enemies] here and slaughter them before me" (Luke 19:11-27).

Over the top. Excessive.

I remind you where the One who told this parable was headed. He came to reclaim his world, and the world received him not (John 1). He kept telling stories, even when we didn't get the point. He freely offered a kingdom not of this world, to all who would open their hands and receive it. Inviting everybody, high and low, to a party without cost. Intruding into the lives of rich and poor. Pronouncing extravagant love for us all.

Over the top. Excessive.

And we turned our backs, refused the invitation, clinched our fists and screamed with one accord, "Too big a risk to be saved by the likes of you!"

The response of the king on a donkey to our violent rejection?

"This is my body, which is given for you. Do this in remembrance of me." In the same way, Jesus took the cup after the meal and said, "This cup is the new covenant by my blood, which is poured out for you" (Luke 22:19-20).

At last, our Lenten journey with Jesus takes us to Jerusalem. Luke uses 21 percent of his Gospel to account for this one last week. In a series of enacted parables, refusing to play it safe, Jesus parades into town on the back of a donkey, as if he owns the place. Some kids recklessly, dangerously hail him as "king." His disciples are clueless; the authorities are edgy.

As for the rest of us, by the end of this week, the crowd who hailed him with "Hosanna!" will cry, "Crucify him!"

Jesus made up all of his parables. Now he acts out of the reality of who he is. To see the truth embodied, in action, confronting the falsehoods of the kingdoms of this world was more than Jerusalem could take. Jesus wasn't crucified for telling stories; he was tortured to death for living them.

Jesus's heroic, politically subversive action through which he cast caution to the wind and stormed Jerusalem? A last supper with his closest friends, who also were his worst betrayers.

"What gives you the right to do these things?" the bigwigs want to know. In response, Jesus (what else?) tells a story. Got time for a tough parable before we have supper?

A certain man planted a vineyard, rented it to tenant farmers, and went on a trip for a long time. When it was time, he sent a servant to collect from the tenants his share of the fruit of the vineyard. But the tenants sent him away, beaten and empty-handed. The man sent another servant. But they beat him, treated him disgracefully, and sent him away empty-handed as well. He sent a third servant. They wounded this servant and threw him out. The owner of the vineyard said, "What should I do? I'll send my son, whom I love dearly. Perhaps they will respect him." But when they saw him, they said to each other, "This is the heir. Let's kill him so the inheritance will be ours." They threw him out of the vineyard and killed him. What will the owner of the vineyard do to them?

(Luke 20:9-15)

When Jesus mentioned "vineyard," everybody in the crowd knew "vineyard" was code for Israel. Isaiah 5 came to their minds:

My loved one had a vineyard on a fertile hillside.
He dug it,

> *cleared away its stones,*
>
> *planted it with excellent vines,*
>
> *built a tower inside it,*
>
> *and dug out a wine vat in it.*

He expected it to grow good grapes—

> *but it grew rotten grapes. . . .*

I'm breaking down its walls,

> *so it will be trampled.*

I'll turn it into a ruin;

> *it won't be pruned or hoed,*
>
> *and thorns and thistles will grow up.*

I will command the clouds not to rain on it.
The vineyard of the LORD of heavenly forces is the house
of Israel,

and the people of Judah are the plantings in which God delighted.

God expected justice, but there was bloodshed.

(*Isaiah 5:1-7*)

Through the prophet Isaiah, God sings a love song about a cherished "vineyard," a song of disappointed love. The Lord cultivated and invested but received "rotten grapes," looked for "justice" and got "bloodshed."

Holy Week, the sad history of God's disappointed love takes a decisive, bloody turn. We didn't listen to the prophets Isaiah, Jeremiah, and Jonah; now we're refusing to hear God's own Son.

The vineyard owner went away "for a long time." Eventually, three emissaries are sent to collect: The first agents are beaten and sent away empty-handed (Luke 20:10). Undeterred by this outrageous rejection, the owner sends a second set of representatives. They are insulted and sent empty away (Luke 20:11). Persevering, a third group of collectors are sent whom the tenants wounded and threw out of the vineyard, in a spiral of escalating violence (Luke 29:12).

Though, "The earth is the Lord's and everything in it, / the world and its inhabitants too" (Psalm 14:1), from the first we've had this violent bent to disregard God's envoys, to treat God's property as if it were ours.

I heard a history lecture, "The Worst Disaster in Human History." Human history took a turn for the worse, according to the speaker, when somewhere back in the distant millennia, we ceased being nomads, settled down, and began planting crops. Agriculture led to somebody staking out a claim, saying, "Mine!"

which resulted in disputes over ownership, which led to wars unceasing, and the world we've got today. Failure to acknowledge Psalm 24:1.

"What will the owner of the vineyard do to them?" Three different, costly, but failed attempts have been made to collect the rent that was the owner's due. Now what?

In the soliloquy of the vineyard owner, Luke takes us right into the very heart of God, enabling us to overhear a colloquy of the Trinity. The owner loves his vinery, investing a great deal in its improvement, graciously overlooking the rent to be past due. The beloved vineyard has been entrusted to the tenants. Stupidly, they have acted as if the vineyard is theirs, reaping the rewards, without accountability, free of charge.

Repeatedly rebuffed, what's the wronged owner to do? Now what?

"I'll send my son, whom I love dearly. Perhaps they will respect him" (Luke 20:13). By sending his only son, surely the renters will regard the son as the owner himself and respond accordingly.

"But when they saw him, they said to each other, 'This is the heir. Let's kill him so the inheritance will be ours.' They threw him out of the vineyard and killed him" (Luke 20:14-15).

"This old guy won't take no for an answer," the tenants scheme. "Killing the son is the only way we can get the old man off our backs and stop him from bugging us about the damned rent. The vineyard will be ours."

Had I the time and you the patience, I could argue that this parable of the Wicked Tenants predicts the birth of the modern world, the dream of a world without God, a realm where there's nobody left to tell us truthful stories we dare not tell ourselves, a domain where we've deluded ourselves into thinking that we can act as we please and nobody will ever come to collect the rent.

The parable does not say that the owner of the vineyard actually destroyed the tenants just as the renters murdered the son. The parable says only what—if there's an ounce of justice in this world—should happen. "The renters have murdered your own son in an attempt to get out of a debt they owe you! Pay them back. Retribution. Justice now!"

What's the Father's response to the long history of refusal and sometimes even violent rejection that God and God's prophets have received from the temporary inhabitants of God's vineyard?

Send the beloved Son.

Standing right in front of us, telling this true story of murderous rejection of the son, is truly the Son.

"When the people heard this, they said, 'May this never happen!'" (Luke 20:16).

Hey, wake up. It's already happened, again and again, has happened and is happening: the owner of the vineyard sent representatives only to have them rebuffed, or worse. Time and again, God's messengers have announced, "The earth is the Lord's and everything in it, / the world and its inhabitants too" (Psalm 24:1), pleading for God's just deserts. Rarely were those messengers respected for telling the truth or welcomed with popular acclaim. Read the Bible, a long story of humanity's rejection of God's unrequited love.

Or perhaps, "May this never happen" is to be taken ironically. Most of the action in the parable of the Wicked Tenants is not consumed with the violent action of the tenants, but with the repeated sending of the owner's servants and then, finally, the son, in the owner's relentless attempts to enable the renters to repent of their past stupidity and at last do what is right.

"I will be your God and you will be my people," God's unilateral determination to love us and to be loved by us is God's story down through the ages (Genesis 17:7; Exodus 6:7; Ezekiel 34:24; 36:28; Jeremiah 7:23; 30:22; 31:33). Read your Bible. Still, if you open your eyes when you gather at God's table on Maundy Thursday you will see again the truth of this parable: This God just won't take no for an answer.

Jesus then, "staring at them," ends the parable with a passage of scripture. The Greek verb *emblepsas*, rendered as "staring," could also be "glared," scowled, glowered. The stone that was the "cornerstone," holding the whole building together, shall be the stone that falls and, in falling, shall crush you (Luke 20:17; quoting Psalm 118:22). The violence you bring against God's messengers shall be your own undoing, says Jesus, glowering.

We thought we were so smart, despoiling creation as if it were ours, mining, building, developing, and using and abusing the world as we please. We've got the whole world in our hands. Climate change is a hoax. Drill, baby, drill.

Are we being crushed by the weight of our own technological, industrial success?

We ran the church as we wanted, erecting impressive buildings and gathering the right sort of people into our sanctified, exclusive club, as if we could do church any way we pleased. Is the decline being suffered by mainline North American Protestantism God's judgment upon us? To us has been given good news of who God is and what God intends and we kept the truth to ourselves, burying it wrapped in a napkin, as if it were our possession rather than God's gift. Is God's gift being taken away from us and given to somebody else?

"What happened?" I asked the district superintendent. "I thought Pleasant Grove was a flourishing church."

"It was," she replied. "About a year ago, one of the long-time members showed up one Sunday with her granddaughter, for whom she has primary responsibility, and her granddaughter's little friend. The granddaughter's friend was Black. Anyway, next Sunday, the little visitor was back, this time with both of her parents.

"That afternoon the grandmother got a couple of telephone calls from fellow members at Pleasant Grove. They said things like, 'You don't think that those people would really be comfortable at our church, do you?' and 'It's fine for somebody to visit, as long as they don't intend to join.' Comments like that.

"Well, the grandmother was brokenhearted. So was her granddaughter. Folks in the congregation chose up sides. Things were said, and not said. Anyway, next month, I'm going to ask you to close Pleasant Grove. I'm hoping we can sell the building to a Pentecostal congregation down the road."

"That's sad," I exclaimed.

Then the district superintendent reflected somberly, "God isn't kind to a disobedient church."

Viewed through the lens of the parable of the Wicked Tenants, I'd say, Woe to a church that thinks the church is theirs.

No wonder, "The legal experts and chief priests wanted to arrest him right then because they knew he had told this parable against them" (Luke 20:19).

It's a story so violent we wish Jesus hadn't told it. Violent, depressing, judgmental. True. Say what you will about the Bible, at least you can't accuse it of being naive or sentimental.

"How come I had to go to the church basement every Wednesday night with AA to learn I'm a sinner?" a recovering alcoholic asked me. Why? Because your pastor is a Methodist sentimentalist who needs to believe—all evidence to the contrary, and in spite of what the Bible says—that you are a nice person who's making progress, able to save yourself by yourself, in no need of being found because you're incapable of being lost.

Rather than tell stories about a God who dares to justify the ungodly (Romans 4:5), a God who eats and drinks with and gives his life for sinners, only sinners, we, the willfully innocent, keep telling ourselves: We are basically good people who, tomorrow, with the right, upbeat motivational talks, could be even better.

Sentimentality cannot account for the Lord who told this violent, truthful story of the Wicked Tenants and then gathered a gaggle of ungodly people around himself at his table the night before tenants of God's vineyard said to ourselves, "Here's the son, let's kill him."

We've got so much sin to own up to. Little wonder why the church insists that Lent last forty days.

What hope is there for people as sentimentally self-deceptive, violent, greedy, and rebellious as we? Hope depends on what the one who owns and loves the vineyard decides to do with us. After murdering the son, is this the last we shall hear from the owner of the vineyard until he comes to destroy? We shall have to wait and see.

The parable of the Wicked Tenants is a preview of Holy Week, the passion of Christ. The Son, come to Jerusalem to collect God's due, shall, after supper in an upper room, indeed be betrayed with a kiss, beaten, cast out of the city, and murdered by a bunch of temporary tenants who act as if the Holy City belongs to them.

"What will the owner of the vineyard do to them?" (Luke 20:15).

That's the question. The owner has every right to be angry with the murderous renters. A high price has been paid for the owner's determination to get the tenants to do the right thing. Violent payback for the violence done would be perfectly understandable. Justice would thereby be served.

Will he "come and destroy those tenants and give the vineyard to others"? (Luke 20:16).

Even knowing how the story ends, the Son steers steadily into the eye of the storm. He won't tell any more parables; his actions will do the talking. The authorities keep attacking him, attempting to entrap him, unanimously reject and refuse him. Yet he keeps walking in the same direction: toward us.

Messengers were sent to us, repeatedly. Finally, the message is delivered by the Son.

What now?

Nobody would blame the owner of the vineyard for destroying the wicked, violent tenants and bringing down justice on their heads. Who would say that's not what they deserve?

Instead, after a string of futile arguments and closing disputations with his refusers, Jesus goes to a meal with his friends (Luke 20:20–22:38). There at the table will be embodied, enacted, the owner of the vineyard's relentless, reckless, risky determination: "I'll send my son, whom I love dearly."

At the Last Supper on Maundy Thursday, he shall promise— even to those who have routinely misunderstood, disobeyed, and refused—the undeserved gift of God's kingdom. At the table before his murder, he shall, in word and deed, refuse our age-old, collective refusal, saying a decisive "No!" to our repeated, stupidly violent no.

Seeking, searching, inviting, giving, suffering, and even dying, all the way to the end, which, because of his unswerving love, may not be the end.

Chapter 6
THE HOST WHO BECOMES THE MEAL

What sort of God's Son would spend his last hours hosting a dinner party for his twelve best friends who were also his most notable betrayers? How is it possible for Almighty God to give himself, body and blood, into the hands of ordinarily violent people like us, loving us even unto death, then returning to the accomplices in his murder, loving them still?

The riddles of Jesus along the road to Jerusalem prepare us for a seat at his table on a Thursday night, a climactic last meal in which Jesus is the host, an enacted riddle of a supper too wonderful for words. For two millennia the church has pondered the mystery of Maundy Thursday, yet we've never exhausted its import. Maybe like any good meal, the Last Supper with Jesus, become The Lord's Supper in the church's practice, is better celebrated than comprehended.

Still, let's try.

Because Jesus is at the table, there's conflict. Even before the meal, threatening conversations swirled outside the dining room. Earlier, you heard Jesus's critics sneer that he ate and drank with sinners, welcoming them to his table. That night, the main malefactor is one of his own disciples:

> *The Festival of Unleavened Bread, which is called Passover, was approaching. The chief priests and the legal experts were looking for a way to kill Jesus, because they were afraid of the people. Then Satan entered Judas, called Iscariot, who was one of the Twelve. He went out and discussed with the chief priests and the officers of the temple guard how he could hand Jesus over to them. They were delighted and arranged payment for him.*
>
> (Luke 22:1-5)

Jesus's response to this maelstrom of satanic conspiracy, betrayal, and bribery? Here, friends, have some bread, take some wine—my battered body, given for you.

As he did on Palm Sunday, Jesus asks for help: "Jesus sent Peter and John with this task: 'Go and prepare for us to eat the Passover meal,'" telling them where to find a room to rent (Luke 22:8-12). To the end, Jesus enlists our aid in setting the table for his salvation of the world, working through his assistants, putting right all things between us and God, celebrated at a supper in a rented room.

Excursus: About the best you can say about me as a pastor is that I'm the one who (in sermons, leadership of the liturgy, teaching and counseling, endurance of the youth retreat, bus trip with the senior citizens, burial of the dead, celebration of marriage) prepares the room and sets the table for Jesus in the hope and faith that he will show up among us. The words that I speak are borrowed, scripted by Jesus. The church where I preach is not mine; it's a rented room. We're temporary tenants. Though the table is set by Jesus's assistants, Jesus condescends to be our host and share meals with us. All I do is to "go and prepare," in the faith that Jesus does the rest.

Luke tells of that Thursday night in a tense, terse account.

When the time came, Jesus took his place at the table, and the apostles joined him. He said to them, "I have earnestly desired [in the Greek, it's literally "I have had yearning on top of yearning"] to eat this Passover with you before I suffer. [Passover: Israel's Fourth of July celebration of the Exodus from enslavement; ironic, since at this very moment some of the religious leaders are collaborating with the pagan overlords to incarcerate one of their fellow Jews.] I tell you, I won't eat it until it is fulfilled in God's kingdom (Luke 22:14-15) [Earlier, Jesus's followers were criticized for their failure to fast and for having too much fun at meals (Luke 5:33-39). Events truly lamentable are about to occur this night. Now's the time for fasting and mourning.]

After taking a cup and giving thanks, he said, "Take this and share it among yourselves [Jesus, forming a community of sharing at the table]. I tell you that from now on I won't drink from the fruit of the vine until God's kingdom has come" (Luke 22:17-18).

[Jesus's ministry began with a forty-day fast, culminates with fasting that won't end until God's kingdom comes, God's will is done.]

After taking the bread and giving thanks, [Jesus] broke it and gave it to them, saying, "This is my body, which is given for you. [Quite a claim for a piece of bread.] Do this in remembrance of me." In the same way, he took the cup after the meal and said, "This cup is the new covenant by my blood, which is poured out for you" (Luke 22:19-20). [Bloodshed linked with a meal.]

[Then the bombshell.]

"But look! My betrayer is with me; his hand is on this table" (Luke 22:21).

An argument broke out among the disciples over which one of them should be regarded as the greatest.

But Jesus said to them, "The kings of the Gentiles rule over their subjects, and those in authority over them are called 'friends of the people.' But that's not the way it will be with you. Instead, the greatest among you must become like a person of lower status and the leader like a servant. So which one is greater, the one who is seated at the table or the one who serves at the table? Isn't it the one who is seated at the table? But I am among you as one who serves" (Luke 22:24-27).

Other Gospels depict the disciples' argument over greatness happening on the road, early in the journey (Mark 9:33-37; Matthew 18:1-5; Luke 9:46-48). Luke, with consummate artistry, places the disciples' greatness dispute here, at the end, at the table.

"Once we get Jesus declared messiah and God's kingdom comes with power, who'll win a seat on the cabinet?" In this argument, those who've been eyewitnesses to Jesus's miracles and have heard all of his parables show that, even at the end, they haven't the foggiest idea what he's been talking about. As Jesus goes forth to serve, the disciples' squabble over greatness certifies them all as betrayers.

Nevertheless, Jesus doesn't give up on them. Just like the seeking shepherd, the searching woman, the persistently inviting host, and the owner of the vineyard, Jesus doesn't stop inviting, teaching, welcoming them just because of their dim-witted failure to understand him. In their obtuseness the disciples thought they were headed toward a culminating victory celebration, not a wake; Jesus continues patiently to teach them anyhow: Haven't you had enough of the kings and kingdoms of this world? In the kingdom that's coming, servants are the ones in charge. "I'm among you as one who serves." To drive home his point, in John's Gospel, servant Jesus gets down on his knees and washes their feet (John 13:1-7).

The last supper is a state banquet inaugurating the governance of King Jesus.

He praises them as "the ones who have continued with me in my trials" (Luke 22:28).

Well, sort of. More or less. In a manner of speaking.

Did Jesus mean that bit about continuing with him in his trials sarcastically? Ironically? Perhaps he meant it charitably, graciously, doggedly determined to see his followers in their best light. Later this evening, when the soldiers come for Jesus and the going gets rough, the limits of our continuing with Jesus in his trials will be apparent. Still, Jesus continues with us.

Jesus then says, "I confer royal power on you just as my Father granted royal power to me. Thus you will eat and drink at my table in my kingdom, and you will sit on thrones overseeing the twelve tribes of Israel" (Luke 22:29-30). To these misunderstanding, half-hearted, undependable, soon-to-be-betraying disciples, Jesus promises a seat at the head table when his kingdom fully comes and we eat and drink at the Great Banquet.

Jesus tells Peter, the Rock, lead disciple, that though Satan has him in his sights, "I have prayed for you that your faith won't fail" (Luke 22:31-32). Peter blurts out, "Lord, I'm ready to go with you, both to prison and to death!" (Luke 22:33).

Jesus correctly responds, in so many words, "Baloney, you'll triple deny me before sunup. Still, you're in my prayers" (Luke 22:34).

Then Jesus turns to the issue of preparation:

"When I sent you out without a wallet, bag, or sandals, you didn't lack anything, did you?"

They said, "Nothing."

Then he said to them, "But now, whoever has a wallet must take it, and likewise a bag. And those who don't own a sword must sell their clothes and buy one. I tell you that this scripture must be fulfilled in relation to me: And he was counted among criminals. Indeed, what's written about me is nearing completion."

They said to him, "Lord, look, here are two swords."

He replied, "Enough of that!"

(Luke 22:35-38)

Back when the journey began, Jesus clearly commanded his followers to travel light: take no bag, purse, or even an extra pair of sandals (Luke 10:4). He reiterated his order here at the table. Disciples venture, "without a wallet, bag, or sandals . . ."

So, in asking, "Any of you have a wallet, bag, or sword?" Jesus is asking, "When I told you to travel without extra baggage or worldly means of self-protection, did you disobey me?"

And his disciples respond, "Sure. Here are two swords that prove our insubordination. Your kingdom may be one of loving, humble service and nonviolent peacefulness; still, just in case you didn't know what you were talking about, we found it prudent to keep a .38 in the glove compartment. Christian realism, and all that."

Seven children or teens are killed with guns every day in the United States. Suicide by gun has gone up 50 percent among American children under the age of seventeen. As I write these words, the North Carolina Republican Party is making good its promise to voters: No background checks or permits required for anybody to carry a concealed handgun.

As Jesus predicted, the hands of his betrayers are on the table. He will be "counted among criminals." Some brigands have broken the laws of the state, others have disobeyed the commands of the one whom they call "Lord." Still others' sin is to boast, "Look at me. I don't even own a handgun. My hands are clean!" Criminals all. Everybody at the Lord's Table eats with dirty hands.

In just a little while, when the soldiers come to arrest Jesus, the disciples ask, "Lord, should we fight with our swords?" (Lord, is now the time we throw off this wimpy love talk, get real, take action, teach 'em a lesson, and whip out our weapons?) One of the disciples, attempting to defend Jesus, pulls out his sword and manages only to nick off a piece of an ear. For this bungled attempt at self-defensive swordplay, Jesus harshly rebukes him: "Stop! No more of this!" (Luke 22:49-51).

Excursus: All Americans believe in self-defense, even those who believe in non-self-defending Jesus. Protection of family is the major rationale for lax handgun laws in America, justification for our having the biggest military budget in the world. Who doesn't believe in self-defense as a supreme good? Jesus, that's who. "Stop! No more of this!" Not one instance of anybody practicing self-defense in Jesus's name in the whole New Testament.

In the drama after supper, when it's very dark, outside the upper room, it's hard to tell the difference between the followers of Jesus and the soldiers of Caesar. Both have swords. When the chips are down, would-be citizens of God's kingdom act like the defenders of the world's kingdoms. Jesus Christ may be our Lord and Savior, but not enough of a lord to accomplish his salvation without our swords.

"Stop! No more of this!" is only one of the things I wish Jesus had not said that night.

Thus ends the Last Supper. After serving his disciples at the table, giving them bread and wine, his body and his blood, after predicting they will all scatter when the going gets rough, after noting and rebuking their sad misunderstanding and outright disobedience, Jesus goes to the Mount of Olives to pray. His disciples fall asleep. (So much for their declarations of "we're with you all the way.") Then the soldiers come. Swords are drawn. It's the end of the road for the Jesus movement. Last act of the drama. Final chapter of the story. Dead end.

You know the bloody injustice, the public humiliation that occurred on Friday after Thursday's meal. Luke reports Calvary without narrative embellishment. Just the facts: clinical, unadorned, unemotional. No need to go into details of the agonies of crucifixion because we know the story all too well; we're citizens of the most violent nation in the world, if you just count the number of Americans murdered by their fellow citizens. We are fast approaching two million Americans incarcerated in this, the Land of the Free, more people reckoned as criminals than any country on earth. Then there's the massacre of Jews by Hamas, the killing and starvation of so many children in Gaza, to say nothing of war in the Ukraine. Even if we are sketchy about some aspects of Jesus's life, we know a great deal about his death, death-dealers as we are. Only the good die young. Incarceration, injustice against innocents, state-sponsored terror, government-run executions, and violent death are commonplace. No need for the Gospels to go into the excruciating detail.

At the table, Jesus had predicted that he would die with criminals. At Calvary, when convicted Jesus hung in agony and infamy, his only conversation partners were two convicts:

> When they arrived at the place called The Skull, they crucified him, along with the criminals, one on his right and the other on his left. Jesus said, "Father, forgive them, for they don't know what they're doing." They drew lots as a way of dividing up his clothing.

The people were standing around watching, but the leaders sneered at him, saying, "He saved others. Let him save himself if he really is the Christ sent from God, the chosen one."

The soldiers also mocked him. They came up to him, offering him sour wine and saying, "If you really are the king of the Jews, save yourself." Above his head was a notice of the formal charge against him. It read "This is the king of the Jews."

One of the criminals hanging next to Jesus insulted him: "Aren't you the Christ? Save yourself and us!"

Responding, the other criminal spoke harshly to him, "Don't you fear God, seeing that you've also been sentenced to die? We are rightly condemned, for we are receiving the appropriate sentence for what we did. But this man has done nothing wrong." Then he said, "Jesus, remember me when you come into your kingdom."

(Luke 23:33-42)

Theologian Karl Barth called this conversation at Calvary the birth of the church. Wherever Jesus is being crucified, surrounded by a bunch of criminals, there's church.

Then, on Sunday evening, first day of the Jewish workweek, day when the disciples were trying to resume normality after the trauma of Calvary, two of them were on their way to the village of Emmaus (Luke 24:3-25). A stranger showed up and joined their conversation.

"What are you talking about as you walk along?" the stranger asked.

"They stopped, their faces downcast. . . . 'Are you the only visitor to Jerusalem who is unaware of the things that have taken place there over the last few days?'" (Luke 24:17-18).

"What things?"

"What planet are you from? Things about Jesus of Nazareth, quite a prophet. But our religious leaders handed him over to be crucified. We had hoped he was the one who would redeem Israel, but the religious leaders care about nobody but themselves, the voters are fickle and Caesar has the army. It was a good road trip while it lasted. We had some memorable meals and heard some great stories. But at the end, there was an election where all were asked for an up or down vote on Jesus. The thief, Barabbas, won the vote. We had hoped, but now, it's ended.

"Some of our women folk came back from his tomb this morning with a cockeyed story of an empty tomb. Said they saw some angels who told them he is alive. A couple of the guys went to the cemetery to check it out. Not a trace of the body. But you know how hysterical some people get when they grieve."

The stranger blurted out, "You foolish people! Your dull minds keep you from believing all that the prophets talked about. Wasn't it necessary for the Christ to suffer these things and then enter into his glory?"

Then starting with Moses and going through all the prophets, the stranger explained every verse that pointed to Jesus as the Christ. True to form, even when Jesus was conducting the Bible study, his disciples were clueless (Luke 24:25-27).

When they got to Emmaus, the disciples said, "Stranger, stay with us. It's nearly evening, and the day is almost over"

(Luke 24:29). There, at the table, still incognito, risen Christ took the bread, blessed and broke it, and gave it to them. In a moment, "Their eyes were opened and they recognized him, but he disappeared from their sight" (Luke 24:31).

The two disciples ran all the way back to Jerusalem where they told the others "what had happened along the road and how Jesus was made known to them as he broke the bread" (Luke 24:35).

His own disciples, his closest friends, couldn't see the risen Jesus, even when he walked alongside them, even when he opened the scriptures to them. It was only when he was at the table with them, took the bread, blessed, broke it, and gave it that their eyes were opened and they saw him in their midst. You remember that same fourfold table action of taking, blessing, breaking, and giving from Jesus's gestures at the so-called Last Supper.

I say "so-called Last Supper" because, as it turned out, Maundy Thursday wasn't the final supper with Jesus after all. What we thought was the last of Jesus turned out to be a prelude to a first supper when "their eyes were opened and they recognized him." Emmaus, birth of the Eucharist.

Surprise. Because God raised crucified Jesus from the dead, the Lord's Supper in your church is not a re-creation of the Last Supper. The Eucharist is not a sad memorial meal commemorating poor, dead, defeated Jesus; it's an Emmaus-inspired victory celebration.

Remember how Jesus said, on Maundy Thursday at his allegedly Last Supper, that he was on his way to his death, the time for lament and fasting had begun? He predicted that he wouldn't again sup with his disciples until they "eat and drink at my table in my kingdom" (Luke 22:30).

At Emmaus, Jesus, strange intruder among us and generous host at the table, in the breaking of bread and drinking of wine, eats and drinks with his people once more, this time as the resurrected Christ. Surprise, the long-awaited God's kingdom is now, here. God's party has begun.

The kingdom of the world has become
the kingdom of our Lord and his Christ,
and he will rule forever and always.
(Revelation 11:15)

Okay. Maybe Christ's kingdom is not completely here in its fullness, but enough of it is here now, to keep us hopeful and faithful now, here. If our eyes could be opened to see the realm of God breaking out among us, there's more kingdom here than we've been able to handle. Jesus may or may not be present, *on the* table, in the blessed bread and wine, but he is always present *at* the table, among the sinners gathered in his name. All are there by invitation only. Jesus is present, relentlessly determined to eat and drink with us forever. Don't tell us; show us. Actions speak louder than words. Have some bread. Take some wine.

Every Sunday is a replay of the supper at Emmaus. Jesus at the table with us once again, as he promised, eating and drinking our way toward the Kingdom. Your church is the way God's kingdom takes up room, establishes a beachhead, a colony of resident aliens amid the failing, failed kingdoms of this world. Every Lord's Supper, Holy Communion, Eucharist, Mass at your church is a foretaste, hors d'oeuvres for the Great Banquet.

We have a sip of blessed wine, eat the bread, and mutter to ourselves, "Well, the women running from the empty tomb on Easter told the truth; he's loose! Our meals with Jesus ain't over till he says it's over."

Whenever your church breaks bread together in Jesus's name, whether on Maundy Thursday Eucharist, or Sunday morning celebration of the Lord's Supper, or even a covered dish supper in the fellowship hall on a Wednesday night, open your eyes, receive the bread, share with your neighbor, the once hard-to-see kingdom of God, described in Jesus's parables, breaking out among us. Come to the party!

One day, the promised Great Banquet of God shall come in its fullness, and we shall feast with one another and Father, Son, and Holy Spirit—not just for a while on Sunday morning or a Thursday evening, but for all eternity. But you don't need to wait until then to have your hunger assuaged. Anytime two or three of us are gathered, and the bread is taken, blessed, broken, and given, Jesus promises, "Just like in the upper room, I'll be there" (Matthew 18:20).

In my second year of seminary, Patsy and I sometimes attended (unenthusiastically) a rather forlorn church on the green in New Haven, right across from the federal courthouse. We were dutifully present at the Maundy Thursday service. What a downer. No more than twenty of us huddled in a cavernous, colonial building, built by New England Puritans. In a dimly lit church, we plodded through the Communion ritual, a lean liturgy left to them by their Puritan forebears. In two hundred years, the ritual had grown stale, sounding stilted as it was mumbled by a pastor counting the days until his retirement.

As we were told, "The body of Christ, broken for you, . . . the blood of Christ, shed for you," a tiny bit of stale bread was offered along with a shot glass-sized plastic cup of grape juice. Jesus once turned water to wine. That Maundy Thursday I saw Jesus's action reversed by a church on its last leg.

"We're giving our lives to lead this?" I said to Patsy, morosely, on our way out of the cold, dark church into an even colder New England night.

A few weeks later, May Day, 1970, in anticipation of the upcoming trial of members of the Black Panthers for torture and murder, throngs of protesters descended upon New Haven. The eyes of the nation were focused upon the federal courthouse for a showdown between radical Yale students (joined by everybody who was anybody in the angry political left) facing off with New Haven police, armed to the teeth and backed up by Richard Nixon's National Guard (praised by everybody on the right). There had been violence and bombs. The university closed. Sewer covers were welded shut to stave off bombings. Apocalypse now.

A group of women from the church, some of the same faithful few who had gathered at the Lord's Table on Maundy Thursday, decided they would keep their church open for anybody to come in from the teargas and the din at the courthouse, just a few yards away. All would be offered sandwiches and lemonade.

Patsy and I spread sandwiches. Maybe I smirked as I smeared the peanut butter and jelly or the pimento cheese. Courageous warriors were out on the street saving America from fascists while in church, we're serving lunch.

Hundreds of people came into the church that day. Twice, we ran out of sandwich fixings and had to go for more. I saw, on one church pew, two National Guard troops, a Connecticut state trooper, and four hippie-looking, long-haired, tie-dyed flower children, talking, laughing even, while they shared our sandwiches.

On the hour, one of the women would climb way up into the colonial pulpit, tap on the microphone, "Is this working?" and then say, "We're so glad you're here today. Let us know how we can be helpful. Please, do be kind to one another, even in your differences. Now, if you are able, join me in a little prayer . . ."

Late that night, at the end of a very long, but amazing day, with the whole town relieved that the violence that was dreaded never came (maybe because of our sandwiches?), I at last sat down on one of the pews next to a guest who looked to be about my age. Nothing else about him looked like me. He asked, looking around as he munched, "What is this place?"

"Church," I answered.

He responded, "This is great pimento cheese."

For the first time that day, I took a bite of one of the peanut butter sandwiches and sipped some of the watered-down lemonade from a plastic cup.

"What kind of sandwich did they give you?" my neighbor asked.

"The body and the blood of Jesus Christ," I answered.

"What's the name of this place?" he asked.

I answered, "The kingdom of God."

Sunday evening after Maundy Thursday, he's back. Showing up (once again) uninvited to his despondent followers, huddled like frightened rabbits behind locked doors (John 20:19). Next thing you know, he's breakfasting with them on the beach (John 21:15-19). Bodily back. Undeniably present. No more parables; just Jesus standing before them, resurrected from the dead, the embodied, seeing-is-believing parable.

Here's a holy riddle: What do you call the place where the one whom we incarcerated and then hung on a cross, dying and coming back from the dead for his betrayers and crucifiers, dining with us, offering himself to us, so determined is he to have us, even us?

Answer: God's kingdom.

What kind of God can be rejected, crucified, dead and buried, only to show up back among his despondent followers, resuming his meals with them? No way to solve that riddle or to make sense of such a God without the help of some stories told by that God.

Heard the one about the extraordinarily reckless, seeking shepherd, the searching woman, the father who waited and then, when his son slinked back home, threw an expensive party? The same father wouldn't stop pleading with the grumbling older brother to come in and join the resurrection fun so determined was the father to have all the family at the table.

Then there was the extravagant farmer who didn't just sit around praying for a good harvest but went forth, wildly to sow, slinging seed all over the world.

Not to mention the frustrated host who kept sending out servants with the invitation to his lavish banquet, telling the whole town, "Come one, come all. There's still room at my table!"

Only a pushy, persistent savior who would invite himself to others' tables, even those who despised him, would defeat our attempted defeat of him by rising from the dead, so determined is he to be at table with us.

We should have known that any preacher who invites himself to the table of Zacchaeus—worst, richest sinner in Jericho—who then went and got crucified for doing so, would rise from the dead, walk right in, sit right down at anybody's table (yes, even ours) and begin telling tales, without being invited to do so, save us from our sin without being asked.

Did you hear the one about Father Abraham telling a rich man in Hades that, if his rich brothers didn't listen to the prophets' warnings, fat chance they would listen to someone come back from the dead?

You are proof that even Abraham was wrong; here you are, pondering the surprise of a God who refuses to be refused, a God who is not only loving, powerful, creative but also determined to have everybody at the table, no matter how much it costs, refusing to take no for an answer.

Let me tell you about the owner of the vineyard who repeatedly sent agents to collect the rent that was his due, only to have them beaten and rejected, finally even sending his own son. That's one relentless, undeterred, determined lover of a vineyard.

Here's the happy ending to that violent vineyard story: The son came back, even when beaten, refused, dead and buried.

The son came right back to God's vineyard after the wicked tenants threw him out and killed him, refusing to be denied his due. He came back, not saying, "Now you will get the punishment you deserve," "Justice must be served," or "It's payback time." Rather he prays, "Father, forgive," then he says and shows us, "I love you, still."

We gave our best shot to get God off our backs, to put an end to the constant inviting, pushy intrusion, sly enticing, relentless giving, and the persistent teaching and storytelling. We tried to shut him up, attempted to silence this itinerant parabolist once and for all by killing him and sealing his body in a tomb.

But God wouldn't take "No!" for our final answer. Unimpressed by our futile refusal, Christ waltzed forth from the tomb, showed up uninvited at their table at Emmaus, returning to the very disciples who disappointed and betrayed him, "As I was saying before I was so rudely interrupted when we were at supper on Thursday."

Maundy Thursday, Good Friday, and then Easter. It ain't over between us and God till God says it's over.

All I've done is to tell you some of the stories of Jesus so that Jesus is enabled to speak for himself: "Let's eat."

One Sunday morning, just before the sappy children's sermon, as the kids came forward, everybody sang by heart that old tune:

> Tell me the stories of Jesus
> I love to hear;
> Things I would ask him to tell me
> If He were here:
> Scenes by the wayside,

> Tales of the sea,
> Stories of Jesus,
> Tell them to me.

"If he were here . . ."? On the basis of our experiences of his real presence at table with us, because of the many riddles he told us about a loving God who keeps turning toward us, whenever we break bread and pass the cup in his name, whenever we tell "the stories of Jesus," we know Jesus *is* here. He can talk his way into any human heart or take over any dinner table conversation.

So on Sunday we say, "Jesus, before we feast on your body and blood, tell us a story."

NOTES

1. Thomas G. Long, *Proclaiming the Parables: Preaching and Teaching the Kingdom of God* (Louisville: Westminster John Knox, 2024).
2. You can find more on Augustine, Julian, Luther, Calvin, and King in Richard Lischer, *Reading the Parables* (Louisville: Westminster John Knox Press, 2014), 151–162.
3. Mary Gauthier, "Mercy Now," on *Mercy Now*, track # 2. Lost Highway Records, 2005.
4. "Hades" may not be what in popular parlance is referred to as "hell."

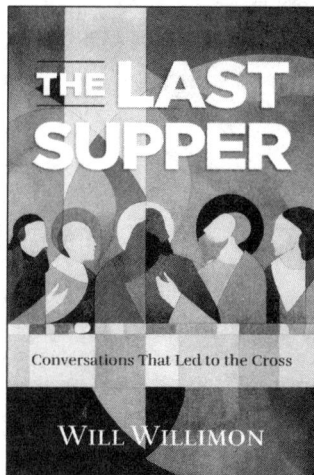